TRINI

TALK

A Dictionary
of Words and Proverbs
of Trinidad & Tobago

Updated and Expanded

Rhona S. Baptiste

A Douens Publication

First published by Caribbean Information Systems &
Services Ltd. Trinidad and Tobago 1994
Second printing by Douens Press 2011

ISBN-13:978-1461148159 (Los Angeles)
ISBN-10:1461148154 (Los Angeles)

Printed in the USA

Dedication

To my grandmother
PAULA PETRONELLA FAIRLEY
who taught us to love our Caribbean heritage

Acknowledgements

I remain grateful to the late Esmond Ramesar whose validation of my attempt to recover the oral heritage in *TRINI TALK – a Dictionary of Words and Proverbs of Trinidad & Tobago* remains deeply appreciated and is therefore still relevant since he wrote it in 1994.

Thanks go out to those family members and friends who aware of the task of compiling our vernacular contributed in their various ways to sustain the on-going effort. Joann Carrington was one of those who researched several of these proverbs with a Tobago bias in an edition that was first published by Inprint Caribbean Ltd. as Dialect-By-Day 1994.

Christopher Morong helped with the book design and pagination but finally it was She Xiuling who completed the final packaging of this edition for CreateSpace.

It was also Xiuling who provided the illustrations from photographs. Try making up your own captions for pictures.

Go ahead enjoy our dialect and proverbs!

Rhona S. Baptiste
2011

Contents

A Melting Pot

Some dates that influenced Trini Talk

The Amerindians, or more correctly the indigenous Peoples of the Americas, are the original inhabitants of the Caribbean. They were neither Americans nor Indians. America is the name for the "new continents" after Amerigo Vespucci, an Italian adventurer, happened upon the Americas. He explored the east coast of South America between 1499 and 1502. Columbus started the myth of the West Indies by thinking that he had reached India.

1498 Genoese Christopher Columbus "stops over" in South Trinidad.

1530 Antonio Sedeño is the first Spanish Governor.

1628 English sailors en route to Brazil pin Union Jack on a tree and claim Tobago.

1655 The Courlanders (Latvians) arrive in Tobago.

1675 The Dutch bring African slaves to plant tobacco in Tobago.

1783 Roume de St. Laurent, a Frenchman, brings in Roman Catholic settlers and slaves.

1797 The British capture Trinidad from Spain.

1806 The Chinese arrive from port of Amoy (Xiamen).

1813 Governor Ralph Woodford orders English language to be used in courts of law.

1834 Abolition of slavery.

1845 First Indentured East Indians arrive on Fatel Rozack.

1847 Madeiran Portuguese arrive.

1851 Lord Harris introduces English into the Primary school system.

1889 Trinidad and Tobago united by British.

1900 Syrian/Lebanese traders arrive in early 20th century.

1956 Dr. Eric Eustace Williams comes to power

1958 West Indians move toward Caribbean statehood with Federation that is short-lived.

1962 Trinidad and Tobago gains Independence.

2010 Trinidad & Tobago elects its first woman prime minister.

Foreword

With the liberalisation of the electronic media, Trinidadians and Tobagonians find themselves exposed to a variety of foreign programmes, some of which are enlightening and broadening. However, we may feel increasingly inundated by an influx of verbal and musical expressions which derive mainly from North America. These elements of a dominant culture, not our own, hasten to impose on us the uni-culture of the late 20th century, and threaten to obliterate expressions which are peculiarly ours.

In the case of trustee of our wealth of language, Rhona Baptiste has devotedly made a collection of familiar words and sayings which she now offers in her *Trini Talk - A Dictionary of Words and Proverbs of Trinidad & Tobago*. The enthusiasm and enjoyment which have accompanied her task are evident, and these are infectiously passed on to us, to be shared with our tourists and overseas friends. In reading through the script, I became quite nostalgic, as proverbs familiar to my childhood appeared or were revived.

The author obviously values the cosmopolitan nature of Trinidad's cultural and linguistic heritage, of which she is a beneficiary. She has drawn widely on Amerindian, French, Spanish, Hindi, African and English sources for phrases. These have become thoroughly Trinidadian, and have passed onto our local *parlance.*

With characteristic imaginativeness, Trinidadians continue to create new words and sayings, to describe new illnesses that afflict us. At the same time, some earlier expressions, used by our foreparents, are being forgotten by us, and are increasingly unknown to our children. Rhona Baptiste has been active in writing and publication for a long time.

We are grateful for this contribution to the preservation of our language inheritance.

Esmond D. Ramesar

Director of Continuing Studies
University of the West Indies
St. Augustine (Trinidad) Campus

Introduction

This dictionary has been around for the past seventeen years!

Since its appearance in 1994 many are the publications that have appeared which appeal to our delight in the sing-song of Trini talk. Perhaps the most popular remains John Mendes' *Cote Ce Cote La* since 1986.

TRINI TALK – a Dictionary of Words and Proverbs of Trinidad & Tobago however, was the natural successor to two years of producing a collection of words and phrases in what was a fun exercise. *365 Trini Words* took the form of a desk calendar in 1993 to be followed by yet another year's desk calendar called *365 More Trini Words* with the same practise-a-word a-day idea. That was with Inprint Caribbean.

Growing up in a household where English (as the Queen would have it) was demanded as the "proper" way to speak, hybrids of the other languages nevertheless found their way into our daily speech.

We children were brought up by a grandmother whose broken English was influenced by broken French from her own grandmother who raised her, and broken Spanish from her father's side of the family.

The result was a patois rich in words in constant evolution that was being changed and exchanged in a school system that had instituted English as the lingua franca.

Tunapuna where we were born and bred, as were so many of the other evolving towns, was a trading place conveniently located at the foothills of the Northern Range along what was to become the East-West corridor. It connects Port of Spain, the capital, with the former Spanish capital of St. Joseph, and with Arima, Sangre Grande, Toco and, farther away, Manzanilla, Mayaro and Guayaguayare.

It was always a meeting place for natives, but since the 19th century the mix of peoples included Spanish–speaking Main-landers especially from Venezuela next door. They were labourers on the cocoa estates of Maracas, Caura and Lopinot valleys where French descendants of the plantocracy and their African slaves were mixing their blood lines and culture with the Scotsmen and other Europeans brought to Trinidad as overseers and tradesmen. Freely mixing into the new melting-pot also were East Indians from the Caroni sugar estates of Orange Grove, Pasea and Streatham Lodge, and Chinese who were staking out business places – shops, rum shops, bakeries, laundries and later restaurants. Portuguese and Syrian/Lebanese were right there too in the trading of dry goods and cloth.

Imagine therefore the cultural effervescence in language as all these newcomers tried to survive alongside each other. And what a marvellous job they did too! Religion, for example, came from the heartland of Africa with its special divinations of Ogun and Shango, across to the European theology of Christianity introduced by the Spanish, French, and British settlers with cross-fertilisation of Hinduism and Islam introduced by the East Indian migrations. Educators were often Irish, French and Canadian in a British school system. A Jewish graveyard exists in the Woodbrook / Mucurapo cemetery that is testimony too that Judaism was once alive and well.

The original settlers among them, the Caribs and Arawaks, had already left behind a legacy of place names like Tunapuna, Tacarigua, Arouca, Arima, Mucurapo, and Naparima along with names of fruits and food. While this is not an academic exercise, it is a continuing record of the fabulous lexicon that we call our vernacular, our dialect, our patois.

How To Pronounce
Trini Words

The best way to learn to talk Trini, the street language of Trinidad and Tobago, is to listen to a native with his/her inflections and intonations.

The end result is a delightful sing-song that is understandably only a step away from the calypso /soca/chutney that is the country's musical art form.

I have tried to develop a simple guide in which the pronunciation next to the word is in parentheses. The word is broken up into its syllable component so the final sound is as close as possible to the Trini word in popular speech. "A" is therefore pronounced as in the alphabet "A for apple" while "ah" is prolonged and "ar" or "a-a" is held even longer.

So, for example, "I want a bat" could become "Ah want ah baht" or "I want a ba-a-t". Never "I want a bet" as the Americans convert their "a" into an "e". Likewise "the" may be pronounced correctly as in standard English "thee" or may be pronounced "dee" or "thuh" or "duh" or "dah".

The "g" at the end of "ing" is usually dropped so "looking" becomes "lookin".

The language is flexible. No pronunciation is given for words and phrases which are pronounced as spelt.

Writing Trini Talk

While the natives speak easily in dialect, it is far from being organised into a standard written form as with the Haitian *Creole* (patois). The result is a perennial conversion of what should be accepted. Take for example *cannes brûlées* from the French meaning cane-burning. Interestingly it has been converted from the acceptable *canboulay* of yesteryear to the *Kambule*.

Newspapers rarely resort to dialect unless the words have become indigenised to the point that they are generally accepted as parts of speech. These include *mas, lime, scrunt, fete* and are examples of speech that have been adopted as acceptable words with precise meanings. Unfortunately there are some words that have been corrupted to the point where "the" for example seems to have got the stamp of approval as "D" from copy writers in advertising agencies. One can see *D Games* or *D Party* in advertisements.

Reference to "artistes" have also become "artists" and is accepted as such in spelling and pronunciation.

The result is that local writers have come around to standardising many of the dialect words, often putting an apostrophe for chopped prefixes or suffixes as in *ah comin' now to go an' hunt de 'gouti*. Words like *gyul, nex* and *jes* along with *ah meh/mih* and *yuh* have become popular.

While there remain differing viewpoints on the spelling of many dialect words, such as *callaloo* and *dhalpuri* and *phulouri*, time will no doubt determine which way the standard will be set as more students of the lexicon formalize the study.

WORDS

A

a b c
Accompanied by "ketch ah crab", it is a popular taunt to belittle one's knowledge or lack of knowledge.
Yuh little brother still in a b c ketch ah crab though!

abir (ah-bee-r)
The red colouring used to splash each other during the Hindu festival of Spring. The ceremony is called Phagwa or Holi.
Ah go ketch mih tail to get dis abir from off mih clothes.

accra (ak-ra)
A local fritter usually made of saltfish (cod fish) and highly seasoned with onions, garlic and hot pepper.
Accra an' float was still de best breakfast yuh coulda find.

advantage
To make use of opportunity; to exploit someone or something.
Dis year Machel really take advantage ah we Carnival!

A from bullfoot
Not having a clue about the subject in question.
You eh know A from bullfoot 'bout what goin' on in de office.

afro
Anything relating to Africa. Also a popular style of haircut.
Since when de boss man Mr. de Silva wearin' Afro?

agouti (ah-goo-tee)
A wild rodent prized as a table delicacy. Drop the "a" to be more Trini when speaking.
Doh forget you could only hunt 'gouti in de hunting season yuh hear!

ah
This is the pronoun "I" and introduces the speaker. It also means "a", the indefinite article.
God bless mih eyesight! Ah so glad to meet mih brother chile!

ah beh beh
An old time way to describe one who makes a fool of himself; a cretin; one who stammers.
Check he out nuh! Monty goin' ah beh beh over dis new chick.

Ah chut!
An exclamation of impatience; a decent form of swearing; could be "ah chuts" too.
Ah chuts man! Mih stocking get a tear from yuh mash-up chair.

ah dey
The local way of replying to your state of well-being, meaning "I'm fine, I'm okay." It may be elaborated to become "ah dey wit dem".
You mean "un dia" in Spanish eh mean "ah dey"?

ah done
I am finished. It is completed. Nothing more to say or do.
You could quarrel all yuh want. You see me? Ah done.

ah eh able / me eh able
This can become 'I eh able' or 'me eh able' and describes incapacity to do something.
Ah eh able with dis ole talk nuh! Is either you comin' or you goin'.

ah fus ah
This introduces a statement and lends emphasis to it.
Ah fus ah love dis gyul yuh hear Mammy!

ah go
This means "I am going to…"
Ah go see yuh.

ah go dead
Not to be taken literally. It means that I have reached the end of
amazement in considering what you are saying or doing.
*Wha yuh sayin'! Marcellin marry Joey for he money? Ah go dead
laffin!*

ah goin' down... to come back
A way of saying the reverse to confirm the point.
*Doh start to eat yet. Wait for me. Ah goin' down de road to come
back.*

ah gorn
I am going ...; a common way to take your leave.
Ah finish... ah done... ah gorn...

ah how
A state of self-pity.
Doh mind how ah lookin' good today nuh, but ah feelin' ah how.

ah mean to say
I really want to tell you... ; used for emphasis.
*Ah mean to say: how you could do me dat! You went and left me
waitin'.*

Ah never see dat! / Ah never see more!
An exclamation to describe a ridiculous situation.
Ah never see dat! Yuh brave enough to come an' ask me for a raise!

ah pass (ah parse)
Leave me out; I'm not in; count me out.
Share out de drinks but doh worry with me. Ah pass.

ajoupa (ah-jou-pa)
The Amerindian term for a hut with thatched roof and tapia or mud
and straw walls.
*All ah want is a little 'joupa, ah good 'oman, an two pickney to
make me happy like pappy.*

all (aarl)
A popular collective noun that introduces any and everything.
All ah all yuh come leh we go down de road.
All kinda ting does happen in dis country.

alloo (ah-loo)
The Hindi word for "potato". An East Indian fritter is called *alloo pie*.
Alloo pie is a good vegetarian dish oui! It tasty for so!

all yuh
A contracted form for 'all of you'. It is frequently used to denote
collectivity.
All yuh have some behaviour nuh! Yuh eh see yuh fadder sick!

alpagatas (al-pa-ga-taz)
A type of footwear from the Spanish Main consisting of a leather sole
with woven tops and backs.
Tie up yuh alpagatas gyul before yuh trip an' fall!

ambakaila
From patois meaning "walk over there" or "get going". It is an old
time chant at the end of a calypso line. This is an excellent
combination of hybrid Spanish, French and English, as *amba* could
have come from the English "to amble", *calle* from the Spanish for
"street", and *là* "over there" from the French.
*Old timers remember dis kaiso when dey used to join in at the end of
"Oh you blooma falling down" and the refrain was – "ambakaila".*

Anansi (ah-nan-see) / nancy story
The name given to the trickster in African folk tales which are
referred to as "nancy stories".
Brer Anansi is de name for the cunning character in de folk tale.

anchaar
A Hindi word for hot pickle of a tropical fruit, a popular
accompaniment with East Indian food.
Oh gorm! Dis mango anchaar tastin' good fuh so!

any time is
This is followed naturally by "Trinidad time" and describes the
natives' relaxed attitude to life.
You go wait all day for dem. Doh forget anytime is Trinidad time!

Apache
This is a spin on the "American Indian" and describes someone with
straight hair and usually of East Indian origin.
No more dougla for Denzil. He goin' around wit a real Apache now!

Apps! (Arps!)
An exclamation of surprise when you catch yourself about to make a
mistake; just in time.
Apps! You wasn't watchin' de cards. Ah beat you dis time!

arepa (ah-rape-ah)
Sometimes shortened to "arepe". It is a corn meal pie stuffed with
seasoned minced meat and deep-fried.
Dem arepa tastin' too sorfee sorfee. Like dey get wet or what!

as man
A brag that denotes superiority; a chauvinist; of macho character.
As man, it eh have one ah allyuh who could chase woman like me!

Ask meh nuh! (Arks mih nuh!)
An exclamation that questions the ridiculousness of the situation. Also
used as "ask mih dis ting nuh!"
*Ask me dis ting nuh! I real chupid waitin' up for he so late every
night.*

assorao (ah-so-rao)
An old saying possibly of Portuguese origin. It means the state of
being harassed or tired.
Gyul, go outside an' play nah. Yuh have me feelin' assorao.

Ay Dios mio! (I-dee-os mee-yo)
An exclamation of dismay of Spanish origin. Translates into "Oh my
God!"
Ay Dios mio! De chile forget he book bag home!

Ay! (A or I or Ai)
Pronounced just so like 'A' or even 'Ai' as an exclamation of despair
or salutation.
Ay little chile! Why you does get me vex so!

Ay Ay! (A-A…) / Ay yai yai! (Ah yah-yai!)
An exclamation of amazement at something unexpected that has
happened; of Spanish origin.
Ay yai yai! We win de match and beat dey tail!

B

baaba
A Hindi word for father or as a form of respect for an old person.
Come nah Baaba, come an sit down here by mih nuh.

bacalao (ba-ca-lao)
Of Portuguese origin, it refers to imported codfish or saltfish.
Long time Pappy use to make a good buljol with nice bacalao an' ting.

bacchanal (bak-ah-nal)
A confusion of events; same as the original meaning for orgy; a mix-up usually referring to distorted communication.
Doh get me involved in dat bacchanal nuh man!

bachac
An ant with a very painful sting; one with a bad temper.
He doh eat nice at all! Him bad like bachac.

bachelor button
The tiny round flower that resembles a button. It comes in variations of pink and purple.
The garden lookin' pretty with all dem bachelor button you plant dey.

back answer
To reply rudely, usually to an older person or to someone in authority.
Doh give mih no back answer or else ah go call you Mooma.

back back
To reverse or to go backwards, for example as when driving a car.
Watch out how you back back in de driveway before you lick down dem post.

back chat
A sassy or cheeky remark; to answer back usually with reference to a child's response when scolded by an adult.
Go to yuh bed right away and stop givin' me back chat.

back pedal
To go back on one's word or to reverse one's decision.
You back pedal now after you say you goin' on de Manzanilla lime?

backra (bak-ra / book-ra)
May be pronounced either way, with a 'y' introduced at times. It means 'poor white' and is well known throughout the Caribbean islands.
Mih neighbour in Tunapuna was a backra from St. Vincent.

backside
The rear end of anything or person more usually that of a female.
Move yuh backside from in front de TV before you block mih vision!

back-to-front
The reverse position of an object, usually a piece of clothing.
Mammy so confuse she put on she blouse back-to-front.

back squeeze
To hold back something from someone, usually money.
When month end come, doh go an back squeeze on mih little pocket change, yuh hear Daddy.

bad
American pop culture has contributed this word that is used to mean the opposite, but in the street language at home it could mean 'very much".
A: *Dat dress have you lookin' like a real bad Mama.*
B: *Yes m' luv I like de colour too bad!*

bad blood
Ill-will or anger between two or more parties.
It have too much bad blood in dis family since de day Pappy dead.

bad drive
To drive dangerously or with little regard for other drivers, not uncommon on local roads.
De young fella give me one bad drive that still have me shakin'.

bad eye
To look crossly at someone.
So why yuh lookin' at me bad eye? What ah do yuh now!

bad feeling(s)
This is usually said in the plural and refers to a state of feeling unwell.
Ah stay straight so ah catch bad feelings so ah done work for de day.

bad john (bard-jon)
A tough character who acts or talks that way.
Is to cut he arse when you see dat little boy playin' bad john.

bad like crab
A state of ill humour.
Doh interfere with dem people. When ah tell yuh dey bad like crab.

bad lucky
The unfortunate state of affairs that may afflict you.
Like ah get bad lucky today since ah see you. Ah lorse mih purse and mih grandmother gold bracelets get tief.

bad mind
A malicious way of thinking; to harbour vindictive feelings for another.
He hold too much bad mind for he in-laws dat is why dey fix he up.

bad talk (*see* **mauvaise langue**)

baigan (by-gan)
A Hindi word for melongene or eggplant.
Cook de baigan wit' curry if yuh want a real good talkaree.

baigan doh back tamadole
An old saying common in the Indo-creole dialect that says that some things are incompatible. In the example given below *tamadole* is tomato.
Jadulal does tell we baigan doh back tamadole.

bake
A native bread prepared with dough that can be fried or roasted.
Coconut bake is de best ting to go with a nice buljol.

bake an' shark
A snack made into a sandwich and popular at beaches.
Hey! Yuh eh hear Jack want to build a tunnel to Maracas to take we for bake an' shark!

balata
A small round milky fruit with brittle shell.
Is a long time since me eh eat ah sweet balata so!

balisier (ba-lee-zay)
A forest flower of the ginger family; the emblem of the People's National Movement.
Yuh coulda know a PNM-ite wit' dem men wearin' de balisier tie.

bamboo band
The old-time method of making music with bamboo and using it as a percussion instrument. This was popular in the thirties and a forerunner to brass and pan.
If you did hear mih grandmother talk about dem bamboo band days!

bamboo tamboo (*see* **tamboo bamboo**)

bambye you go see
An old dialect phrase meaning "watch out you'll see what's going to happen!"
He too ole fuh she. Dey lookin' happy now but bambye you go see am.

bamsee/bumpsee/battee
These are all variations on backside or bottom or rear end.
If you see dem woman and man now with dem KFC bamsee!

band (ban)
Any group of people who come together to play 'mas in the streets on Carnival days.
Come quick nuh Mama. Yuh eh see de band passin'.

bandara
A Hindi word for a pot which is used for pressure-cooking channa or chickpeas.
Ay boy, Jadu say to use de bandara pot instead of de fancy pressure cooker or else de channa go lack good texture for dem doubles.

Band of the Year
The Carnival band that takes first place in the annual masquerade competition.
It was names like George Bailey, Stephen Lee Heung, Hart, Wayne Berkley and Peter Minshall dat always did take Band of the Year.

bandit
Recent term to describe Low Life; a thief; anyone in criminal activity.
It did'na used to have all dem bandit an' dem in de old days nuh man!

band yuh jaw/belly
Another way of saying 'bite the bullet'. Taking steps in preparation for hard times ahead.
You better band yuh jaw with all dis talk 'bout money an' how dem spendin' an' wastin' it.

banjo
A small stringed instrument similar to a guitar, popular in parang music.
If you did hear sweet music when Uncle Ton Ton uses to play dat banjo!

barbadine (bar-ba-deen)
A large fruit borne on a vine and popular for making drinks and ice cream.
Guess what ah see in a Korean shop in Brooklyn? Is barbadine if you please.

barra (bah-rah)
The East Indian dough filled with channa (chickpeas) or dhal (split peas) and popular as a snack; that is now known as doubles.
Barra is what dey used to sell long time in de school yard not doubles.

barrack yard
Living quarters named because of its long wooden military appearance. It is associated with bawdy behaviour of its occupants and was the popular setting of many West Indian novels.
Yuh getting' on like ah real barrack yard woman!

bat (b-a-a-t)
A derogatory term used to describe a woman of loose morals.
Doh call she ah bat. You eh go like nobody to call yuh sister dat.

bat an ball
A game popular with youngsters and involving any two moving objects.
Coconut stalk does make a good bat for de bat an ball game by de beach.

batchac from Bad Jack (*see* bachac)

batchie (ba-chee)
Any small living quarters occupied by a single occupant; a bachelor's quarters.
When you see ah done work ah goin' home to mih little batchie.

batimamselle (ba-tee-mam-zel)
A dragonfly or damselfly; beautifully slender insect with two pairs of diaphanous wings. Possibly from patois *belle petite mademoiselle*.
Look how she dress up and walkin' down de road like a little batimamselle.

battle axe (batul-ax)
Someone who is loud-mouthed and ready to pick a fight; abrasive and of large girth.
Watch how you gettin' on like dat battle-axe Cousin Elvira.

batwan
A Hindi word to describe a pre-wedding night when huge preparations take place in cooking for the event.
If you see how many of Parwattee friends come to help she cook at she sister' batwan down in Chinapoo.

bawl
To cry out or shout or scream. "To bawl out" is to upbraid someone publicly so as to make him or her ashamed.
Nowadays yuh frighten to bawl out dese young people as all ah dem does have attitude.

bay hay (bey hey)
An old description of the last child.
You eh know Mammy always use to call Ray she bay hay.

Bazil
A male name; a fragrant herb; Bazil is also known as the Grim Reaper.
He come so maigre like he jes' waitin' for Basil to come get he.

bazodee
To be in a state of stupidity, or confusion; in a daze.
The news dat he wife just make de chile had he bazodee.

beast (beese)
Any Carnival character or attitude depicting the devil and/or his imps. However it could be used to describe a nice-looking woman.
You eh see dah beast passin' in front de pizza shop? She nice too bad.

beat
To overdo something; repetitious; often used as in " to beat the daylight out of something or someone".
She beatin' de daylight out of dat dress.

beat pan
The action of making music on steel drums. There are several sections depending on the tuning of the particular pan, for example the guitar pan, the bass and tenor pan.
She does work in de bank by day but does beat pan by night.

beat up
Old and weathered; unusable.
He come with he ole beat up self to take me out in he beat up ole Flintstone car.

beatin' yuh own drum an dancin'
To sing out your own praises.
He always beatin' he own drum an' dancin' to it.

bee bop
A skimpy hat and style reminiscent of the fifties; it was also a popular dance step at the time.
Where yuh get dat ole bee bop cap from? Like you raid yuh grandfadder closet!

bégayer (bey-gay-yae)
Of French patois origin. To stammer or stutter in replying.
He get nervous when she confront him wit de news so he begin to bégayer.

behin' God back
Any distance that cannot be easily described; too far for comfort.
You mean I have to drop you up in Santa Cruz way behin' God back!

behind de bridge
The densely populated urban area east of Dry River in Port of Spain.
De MP lady was proud to say she come from behin' de bridge.

beke negre (bey-key-neg)
A half-white or light-skinned person of African descent; a mulatto. It originates from patois or creole common in Caribbean region.
Pass for white whey? You cyar see she's a beke-nege.

bèlè (bel-leh)
A song or ballad. It is also a delicate dance of French creole origin and brought to a fine art by the African slaves.
De audience at Queen's Hall enjoyed de bèlè too bad.

belly (bel-lee)
Having a lot of nerve or guts to act accordingly.
You mus' have plenty belly to stay in dat kind of situation.

belly full
A large mango that is filling but not particularly tasty.
Dat mango is ah real belly full just like its name.

bene balls (bay-nay balls)
A candy native to Tobago. It is made of tiny sesame-like seeds held together in a hardened caramel. *Bene* is said to have been introduced from Africa; it is a hardy annual plant. The seeds are parched.
Rufus doh forget to bring back some bene balls from Tobago for mih eh!

besay down (bay-say dong)
From the French *baiser,* "to kiss". In dialect it has come to mean to move the waist sideways and down in provocative dance movement.
Come leh we besay down to dis tune.

betaa (bey-taa)
A Hindi word used affectionately and meaning "son" or "child".
Behave good nah betaa. Yuh have everybody lookin' at yuh.

betee (bey-tee)
A Hindi word meaning "daughter" and often used as term of endearment.
Betee come help mih carry dis bucket outside in de yard.

better yuhself
To improve your status; to move up in the world.
So you finally goin' away to better yuhself in Florida!

bettie goatie (beh-tee goat-ee)
A challenge that brags or dares the other person to respond; a taunt.
Bettie goatee, mih Daddy stronger dan yuh Daddy.

bhagi (bah-gee)
A local spinach that shrinks when cooked, which makes a tasty
vegetarian dish. It is used creatively to describe a compromising
attitude.
If you see how she boil down like bhagi when she lorse de big wuk.

bhajan (bah-jhan)
A Hindi word that describes a hymn sung at prayer meetings.
Pundit Narine does sing de bhagan at all we prayers.

bhowjee (bow-gee)
The Hindi word for "brother's wife" or "sister-in-law".
Stop frettin' nah gyal an' go an' make up with bhowjee.

Biche (bee-sh)
The name of a country district in east Trinidad; "to break biche"
means to skip school; to play truant.
Ah sendin' him to spend holidays by mih sister in Biche.

biddim bim (bee-dim-bim)
This is a particular jest for a male whose long pants fall short of his
ankle.
Boy, which tailor make you dem biddim bims?

big belly doon doon
A joke or taunt at someone who is overweight and paunchy.
Whey yuh pushin' yuhself goin' with yuh big belly doon doon self?

big mouth (big mout)
Someone who talks a lot and noisily usually divulging someone else's
secrets and making a nuisance of him/herself.
Dat member of Parliament big mout for spite!

big pappy (big pap-ee)
Someone elevated to a high position in society; an assumed attitude of greatness; an authoritative figure.
You stop writin' blogs since you turn big pappy in de government!

big up
Totally American slang adapted in common radio parlance to mean "make important" or "to talk up on behalf of".
An doh forget to big up mih son Darren on yuh radio programme as is his birthday today.

bite up
Someone with an irritable or quarrelsome disposition with a resulting hostile attitude.
One little let down an' is so yuh getting on bite up, bite up?

black cake
A unique fruity caramel cake made of mixed fruit soaked in cherry brandy and rum months before Christmas.
I post mih black cake to Natalie and yuh know like dem Customs people me eh know whey - tief it jes so!

black is white
To speak out to the point; as a matter-of-fact.
I tell she black is white to leave de man and go find a wuk.

blag
From the French word *blaguer,* to tease or jest. It is used however to mean idle chatter, otherwise known as *ole talk* in which natives take delight.
Ah goin' down de road by neighbour Nola to blag a little.

blank
To leave out; to omit or by-pass; to snub.
She blank mih at de fete all night. You know de gyul lef mih an gorn wit she friends!

bleach (bleesh)
To leave clothes outside to whiten in hot sun on stones heaped in the backyard for that purpose.
Put de man clothes on de bleach quick to catch de sun.

bless
From the French word *blesser,* "to wound" or "to hurt". In dialect it means a lash, a curse.
She have so much bad luck she mus' be bless!

blinkin'
A way to swear.
Me cyar wait in dat blinkin' traffic jam!

blight
Describes a continuing state of bad luck, or the person associated with it.
Keep she far from mih plants. She go put ah blight by jes watchin' dem!

bling
American slang, introduced through music and film, which describes an ostentatious lifestyle among youths.
Dem young people like too much ah bling.

blocko
A street party made popular with the advent of dee jays.
De blocko causin' real traffic horrors an' doh talk 'bout de noise!

blookas (bloo-kaz)
Ugly, over-sized footwear.
Marcia, where yuh goin' wit' dem blookas? Dey lookin' jokey!

bloomers (bloo-maz)
The oversized underpants that women wore in the old days.
Listen to dis ole chant: 'Oh Lard she bloomers fallin' down' an you must sing out 'Ambakaila'.

bloomin' (*see* **blinkin'**)

bloomin' France
The state of being dismissed far away from the speaker; decent way to swear.
What de bloomin' France you tellin' me 'bout yuh lorse yuh wuk so no chile maintenance dis month!

blow away (blo 'way)
Another way to say 'get lost'.
Wish ah could tell some ah dem politicians to blo 'way.

blowhard (blo hard)
Someone who pretends to do but does not deliver what is promised.
Ay boy! I could name plenty blowhard on both sides ah de government.

blow off (blo-orf)
Children stick their thumbs on cheeks and wave vigorously to further make the point that they are not talking to each other.
Ah goin' to blow off wit' yuh right now for tiefin' mih sweetie.

blow yuh mind (blo yuh mine)
Someone or something that is breath-taking; out of this world; unbelievable.
Dat movie go blow yuh mind. It have so much ting to make you tink!

Blue Devil
A breed of imps that appear on j'ouvert at Carnival. They are painted blue with tiny horns and wire tails to terrorize onlookers.
Is Johnny Lee whey used to bring out ah good Blue Devil side round de savannah every year.

blue duck / blue dock (bloo duk)
The name given to denim of yesteryear and popular among masqueraders for Monday mas when playing sailor at Carnival.
Mammie say is she who introduce blue duck to go to work in high style.

blue food
Any ground provision, in particular blue yam, dasheen and cush-cush, regarded as a staple.
De Minister of Tourism should put blue food on de national menu.

blue jean(s)
A tight-fitting denim pants; also the name for the blue-gray Tanager.
Yuh talkin 'bout Granny old blue jeans or dem little birds on de window-sill?

bobo foot
One who has bad skin, with special reference to marks on the legs usually as a result of childhood eczemas.
She steppin' in style but check out de bobo foot nah!

bobol (boh-bol)
The state of fixing something so as to profit dishonestly; a scheme or plot to defraud; corruption; crooked transactions.
When ah tell yuh it have bobol in high places in dis country!

bobolee
Effigy of Judas beaten in the streets on Good Friday as remnant of old Christian ritual for betrayal of Christ and subsequent crucifixion.
Doh treat me like no Good Friday bobolee.

bobotay
Incredibly stupid.
You mean she go marry dat bobotay!

boca funcia (bo-ka foon-see-ah)
The cocoa 'pagnol version that refers to someone with a twisted mouth.
He tink he so nice wit' he ole boca funcia self.

boderation (bod-ah-ray-shun)
A troublesome person or thing; or simply a state of disturbance.
Ah stop fixin' dis car yes. It givin' meh too much boderation.

bodi (bo-dee)
A popular green bean also called stringed bean that is good in curry or stewed with meat or saltfish.
Ah feelin' to eat a little curry bodi with mih blue food today.

boil down (boil dong)
To cool oneself or one's temper; a state of regaining one's composure.
Look how she boil down like baghi after flarin' up an cussin' mih.

bois (bwa)
From the French meaning "wood" or "stick", it refers to the instrument used in stick-fighting long ago. It can also mean "licks".
When dem youth misbehavin' is to give dem plenty bois in dey tail!

bois bandé (bwa ban-day)
It means "stretched wood" and is of French origin. A bark used as an aphrodisiac and it is believed to enhance sexual prowess.
Put a little piece a bois bandé in meh drink. Dat go fix meh up good.

bois canot (bwa can-no)
A tree with crisp curled leaves when dried, which along with its bark and roots are used for making medicinal teas for colds and snakebite. The French for "wood" is *bois* and *canot* is "small boat".
Make sure an' leave de bois canot tree on de estate yuh hear!

bois flo (bwa flo)
A woody tree that is a member of the silk-cotton family. Seeds with downy hairs lend themselves to dispersal and to stuffing pillows.
It eh have nutten like dem long-time bois flo pillows eh gyul!

bold face (bole-face)
The ultimate in brass; effrontery.
De bold face vendor sell meh rotten fruit and den vex ah tell she.

bolokshus (boh-lok-shus)
Anyone large and ungainly.
She bring she old bolokshus self to de party and den park up sheself right dey by de kitchen.

bonda poule (bon-da poule)
Literally "fowl mess heap" from the French. An untidy patching of a garment.
Do de wuk neat. Doh make no bonda poule on de dress hem yuh hear!

Bon Dieu Seigneur! (boh dieh seh yieh)
An exclamation of French origin that means "Good God Saviour!"
Ay Bon Dieu Seigneur! Look what dat dog do wit' mih new shoes!

bong navel
Originally this came from "bound navel" and refers to a protruding navel caused by excessive crying as a baby.
Doh trouble yuhself. De chile bong navel will go dong when yuh ban' it.

bongo
An African drum; dance steps to particular kind of drumming heard at wakes or other village ceremonies.
Me cyar never forget de bongo drums an dem at Ma an' Pa Jack weddin' up in Toco.

bong to
"Bound to" in its original state. This is used for emphasis.
Ah bong to go to church every Good Friday in Lent.

boo
This is a derisive noise or term aimed at someone who is unpopular. It can also describe bad news.
When ah tell yuh dat man boo. He doh spend a cent when we go out.

boo boo man
A bogey man; someone fabricated for scaring little children away from doing something wrong.
Long time parents used to do more harm dan good wit' dose threats dat de boo boo man comin' to get yuh.

boo boo nan nai
A way to describe someone who is timid; a shy person; a country bookie.
Way yuh get dat boo boo nan nai chile from!

boof calalay boof (boof ka lay-lay boof)
A childish taunt calculated to demoralize the opponent.
Stop gettin' orn chupid nuh only sayin' boof calalay boof.

book keepress (book-kee-priss)
A female who is an accountant or book-keeper.
Grannie say she friend uses to be a bookkeepress at Miller's Store on Frederick Street.

bootoo
The short stick or baton used by police officers.
Dem days fuh bootoo done oui! Is only gun dem police usin' now.

born Trini
A person who considers him/herself to be a native Trinidadian and lays claim to being the most irrepressible person on earth.
Is only ah born Trini could give an take heckle so.

bosee back (bo-see bak)
A humped or deformed back. A derogatory term used to ridicule.
Yuh want to give meh a bosee back totin' dis bunch of fig!

botay
To dance with wide sweeping movements from side to side, reminiscent of the fifties.
He use to be king of de botay long time but look at he now!

bottle an' spoon (bot-tul an spoon)
Kitchen utensils that are used as improvised musical instruments.
Is only bottle an' spoon now to complete dis Maracas lime.

bottle dance
The art of dancing on broken bottles.
He grandfadder used to make a livin' doin' bottle dance at Miramar Nite Club.

bouchet (boo-shet)
It refers to the physical condition to which innards "drop" in the abdomen.
Ah eh feelin' so good nuh. Like mih bouchet drop.

boughie (bowgee)
A Hindi word for sister-in-law.
Come nah, boughie, an' help meh grind de massala.

bounce up
To meet someone unexpectedly, on the street or at a party.
Lo and behold ah bounce up Miss Lady an' she sweet man at de fete.

box cart
An original means of transport in country districts and a play cart for youngsters.
Leh we have a box cart race like long time nuh!

Bradap(s)!
Used in the singular or plural form to describe a falling motion. An exclamation of surprise.
Bradap! De chile fall down an' bruise she leg on yuh chupid skateboard.

bragadosho
A braggart; someone who shows off; a person who tries hard to impress; from the English word "braggadocio".
Dat bragadosho always tellin' mih mudder how much money he does make.

bram
A raucous party or fete.
If yuh eh look sharp dis decent fete go turn into a reel bram.

bramble (bram-bul)
To talk around the point without getting to it.
He tink he smart when he bramble yuh 'bout payin' back de loan.

brass face (*see* **bold face**)

braver danger (bra-vay dan-jay)
Of French origin, it means "to defy danger". Someone who displays fearlessness; putting on a brave appearance.
Doh play no braver danger an' stay by yuhself in dis lonely place.

break away
To break away from the normal. It is used especially with reference to dancing with abandon.
Everybody break away an' doh want to leave de fete.

break biche (break beesh)
To miss school deliberately opting for the beach or shopping.
Long time teachers used to cut yuh tail if yuh break biche.

breds / bro
Used to relate to a "brother" or someone recognized as being like you. Also known as "bredda man".
Look here nuh breds. Both ah we in de same khaki pants. We have to find a wuk.

broke
To find yourself without a cent; penniless; state of poverty.
Look how ah find mihself well broke dis month end!

broko foot
One who walks lopsidedly or with a limp; injured or deformed leg.
Go an' help de broko foot man to cross de road nah boy!

broughtupsy (braut-up-see)
The manner in which a person is well-bred and displays good
breeding.
If yuh see how we High Commissioner to UK lookin' nice too bad!
Is he good broughtupsy.

brown skin
A person with a brown complexion and popularized in the ole time
calypso "Brown skin girl stay home and mind baby".
Look she dey. Is de same brown skin gyul ah jump up wit' in de ole
mas band.

bubulups (boo-buh-lups)
Someone who is fat and overweight. A derogatory term referring to
one's size and appearance.
Dey say is too much fas' food dat have we people so big an'
bubulups.

budow (buh-dow)
To be "in budow" means to be involved with something or someone.
Used in the negative.
Doh let she fool you. She eh in budow wit' he.

buff (boof)
A rebuff; a response that causes the person addressed to feel slighted;
to diss or to reprimand.
Mih fadder will good buff mih for comin' home so late.

buffalypso (buf-ah-lip-so)
An indigenous breed of animal; a type of buffalo developed in
Trindad by Dr. Steve Bennett. *Lypso* pays tribute to the term
"calypso".
The buffalypso is a true Trini-to-de-bone animal.

buljol (bool-jawl)
A local dish made with salted codfish and seasoned with tomato, onions, hot pepper, oil and vinegar.
Oh gorm! Dis buljol goin' good wit' de coconut bake!

bull pistle (bull pis-sul)
The name given to a whip made of dried leather tongs and used long ago to drive the cattle herd.
De criminal an' dem need good bull pistle to straighten dem out.

bum a ride
To request or beg transport from someone.
Look nah man ah want to bum ah ride to go down town.

bum bum (*see* **bamsee**)

bun bun (bon bon)
The burnt layer of rice cooked up like pelau that sticks to the pot.
Take some pelau but leave de bun bun fuh me.

burrokeet (buh-row-keet)
From the Spanish *burroquito*, "little donkey". An old time carnival character with a donkey's head and a heavily padded rear end.
Gyul all dem clothes jes makin' yuh look like a burrokeet.

bus' de mark
To "burst the mark"; to bring something unexpectedly out in the open; first with the news; originated from the game of chance called *whe-whe*.
Wait till ah bus' de mark in de meeting 'bout wha really goin' on!

'buse up / 'buse down / 'buse comin' and goin'
From the English word "abuse"; to emphasise the degree of dressing down.
When ah tell yuh ah good 'buse she up for bad-talking mih.

bush bath
Used when someone takes a bath with a pail of water mixed with bush and herbs. It is believed to cool the body when ill, or more likely to get rid of any blight.
Some ah we so blight we need ah good bush bath.

bush tea
A hot drink brewed from herbs used for medicinal purposes. It is usally associated with country people.
Ah ent shame to say we uses to drink bush tea with orange peel an' lemon leaves.

bus it
To get out of a place fast.
If yuh see how she bus it outta here when he mother drive up in de garage.

buss ass
Literally "to burst ass".To lose terribly or to beat someone else as in a game or fight.
In Santo Domingo when we swim team was winning we change we chant from buss ass to busso arsso.

buss up shut
Paratha roti; originates from "burst up shirt" since it aptly decribes the soft flaky texture of the dough served with curry.
It eh have nutten nowhere like a river lime with good curry duck an buss up shut.

But how yuh mean!
An exclamation, or a statement that agrees with a situation.
But how yuh mean! Ah cyar miss de boy weddin' fuh nothing!

But look at mih cross!
The questionable state when one finds oneself in an unfortunate or unexpected situation.
But look at mih cross! Yuh comin' to stay wit' meh for six weeks! Yuh mad or what!

C

ca ca dent (*see* **ka ka dent**)

ca ca yank (*see* **ka ka yank**)

cacapool (ka ka pool)
It originates from the patois meaning "fowl mess". Used to describe the worst grade of alcohol.
Every Saturday night he does fin' heself in Chin rumshop to drink out de cacapool rum.

caimite (kai-mit)
A purple fruit borne on a large tree; also known as star apple.
Dis caimite sweet an' milky too bad!

calabash (ka-la-bash)
A large round fruit used as a gourd or for other decorative pieces when dried; often cited to taunt a person with large head.
Country people does still use de calabash to tote water.

calaboose (ka-la-boose)
From the Spanish *calaboza,* "gaol".
All dem criminal terrorist is to throw dey tail in de calaboose.

calinda (ka-lin-da)
An African chant that accompanies stick-fighting.
De show at Queen's Hall was featurin' calinda an' ting.

callaloo (ka-la-loo)
A Trinidadian dish made with young dasheen bush leaves, ochroes and crab.
Nutten does taste as great as mih mother callaloo.

call dat George
It signals that you are finished with someone or something; washing your hands off the matter.
Ah cleanin' mih desk, ah leavin' de building an' ah go call dat George until after de holidays.

calpet (kal-pet)
A blow on the head.
Man behave yuh self before ah hit yuh one calpet.

calypso (ka-lip-so)
A unique art form of song and dance native to Trinidad and Tobago. It is also known as kaiso.
Hear nah man! Calypso is a kinda media that does tell a true story.

calypsonian
The singer who delivers the message through the medium of calypso.
Calypsonian always have plenty to sing 'bout dem leaders an' de society.

calypso tent
The place where the season's crop of new songs are presented by a group of calypsoninans.
Ah hittin' all de calypso tents dis year.

camboulay (kam-bu-lay) / canboulay
From the French *cannes brulées*, "burnt cane" or "cane-burning". It gave rise to a celebration among the sugarcane workers at the end of the crop-harvesting season.
Me eh have no idea why dem change de spellin' of "camboulay" to "kanbule".

cane row (kane ro)
An African hairstyle in which the strands are plaited closely and neatly.
She have she hair plait up in nice cane row.

capra (ka-pra)
An East Indian style of male dress when fabric is wrapped into loose-fitting trousers.
Is Christopher Pinheiro who make capra mainstream high fashion.

caprice (ka-preesh)
To ramble around something; to take a roundabout way to say or to get out of a position. From the French *caprice*, meaning whimsical.
At dis stage of de game doh try a caprice on mih eh.

caraille (ka-rai-lee)
The fruit of a vine used for medicinal purposes. It is quite bitter but a popular vegetable in the countryside.
Drain off de water from de caraille as it real bitter before fryin' it up.

Carajo! (ka-ra-ho)
Introduced by Venezuelan peons and used to curse or swear, meaning "Oh hell!" or "Dammit!" It is followed by *pendejo*, "bull shit" in Spanish.
Carajo! Ah lorse de lottery again dis week!

cargoo (ka-goo)
The state of being tired and listless; looking and feeling depressed and unable to cope.
Woman, cheer up and stop feelin' cargoo nuh! Man go man dey!

Carib
The original inhabitant of South America and the Caribbean. It is also the name of a popular beer.
Ah is a true Carib descendant who does drink Carib. Mih family come from Arima.

Carnival
From the Latin *carne vale* meaning "farewell to the flesh" during the pre-Lenten period, namely the Monday and Tuesday before Ash Wednesday. It was introduced by the French plantocracy in the 1700s, and was a period of self-indulgence in song, food and dance.
Trinidad Carnival is still de Greatest Show on Earth! We must stop too much politics an' greed from spoilin' it.

carré (ka-ray)
From the French word *carré* meaning square off as during a stick fight.
Man, doh carré for meh nuh or else ah go call de police.

cascabel (kas-ka-bel)
A poisonous snake, yellow and green in colour, unafraid to retreat when threatened.
Ah wouldn't like to meet a cascabel on dis hike nuh man!

cascadura (kas-ka-doo-ra)
A native swamp fish that is scaly and sweet, usually cooked in curry.
Legend say dat once you eat de cascadura you bound to return to we country.

Case!
That's it! This is it! I'm finished! It's all over! Any of these exclamations make the point. It is also used creatively like "Caso blanco!" no doubt a pun on the Venezuelan *queso blanco* for white cheese.
Case! Ah tell yuh ah was goin' to win de game.

cashew
A fruit better known for its seed than for its astringent flavour.
Ah didn't know he coulda make a good cashew wine from de fruit!

cassava bread
An indigenous staple in South America and the Caribbean, made from the flour of the root tuber.
Mih Grandma did teach mih how to make farine an' cssava bread.

Castillian (kas-tay-yan)
Music and dance representative of the early Venezuelan settlers.
Yuh shoulda see how dem children dancin' Castillian like de real Spanish!

catch a geege (ketch ah geege)
To get excited about an idea; to become restless.
De nex' ting ah know he catch a geege an' say he goin' Sando.

catching hell (ketchin' hell)
This is the same as "catchin' mih nen nen" which means that you are having a difficult time eating, sleeping, and working.
Boy since Mary lef me ah catchin' hell to stay alive.

catch yuh nen nen
Nen nen is the word for godmother. However to "catch yuh nen nen" is to have difficulty accomplishing something.
Yeah boy, go an' lef Dolsie an' see how yuh go catch yuh nen nen to get she to take you back.

cat in bag
To get something that you have not bargained for; to risk buying something without knowing the details of your purchase.
When ah drive home de car from Bamboo ah realise that ah did buy cat in bag.

catspraddle (kat-spra-dul)
To tumble down or fall face downward with limbs spread out.
Watch yuh doh go an' catspraddle on dat slippery floor.

cattle boil (cat-tul boil)
A pimple or swelling on the eyelid which is said to develop when you give something away and then take it back.
Yuh take back de ring you give she so what you expect de cattle boil to do!

cavali (ka-val-lee) (coo-val-lee)
A popular sea fish.
Dis cavali go taste good in curry or fry up.

centipede (san-tee-pee)
A many-legged poisonous creature common in the tropics. It also describes a hot-tempered person.
Watch out for she. She bad like centipede!

cerise (see-rees)
A small purple fruit with many seeds in yellow pulp. It is usually rolled to soften before eating.
Like ah doh see plenty cerise trees growin' 'round here again!

cha siu kai fan
A Cantonese dish popular with Trinidadians; it is made of Chinese-flavoured barbecue pork and chicken, and served on rice.
When ah went Hong Kong all ah wanted to eat was cha siu kai fan but it eh nutten like we own.

chac chac (shak-shak)
Known in Africa as the "shara shara" and in Brazil as the "sha sha";
gourd filled with beads or seeds used to shake off evil spirits during
divination ceremonies. It is now a rhythm keeper also called
"maracas" in South America and the Caribbean.
It eh have no good parang band without a good chac chac player.

Chaconia (sha-coh-nee-ah)
The national flower of Trinidad and Tobago named in honour of
Spanish Governor Don José Maria Chacon. It is also the name of a
national award.
It eh have nothin' prettier dan a double chaconia flowers.

channa
A dried round pea that is tasty either boiled, fried and salted, or
curried. It is also known as chick peas.
*Is channa dat make up de staple for a good breakfast wit' doubles
an' coconut water.*

chantwell
From the French for "singer of ballads". Chantwells were the
predecessors of calypsonians.
Is de chantwell and dem who was de real master of picong.

charge up
The state of bliss after a few drinks too many.
Doh trouble he at all. Whey you see he dey he well charge up.

chataigne (sha-tyne)
A variety of breadfruit with chestnut-like seeds. When boiled and
salted it can cause much flatulence when eaten.
Boy wha is dat! Like yuh eat plenty chataigne today!

chennet
A fruit known as *guinep* elsewhere in the Caribbean. It is round and
green with a soft pink pulp and brittle shell. It is related to the Chinese
lychee and dragon eye fruits of the Sapindaceae or Soapberry family.
Dem chennet sweet for so but de tree so blinkin' high!

cheups (*see* steups)

cheveux tac tac (shee-vay-tak-tak)
From the French patois meaning "hard hair", it refers to a thick unruly head of hair.
Yuh would'na believe dis chile born wit' straight hair, now it gorn cheveux tac tac.

chicanier (shee-kan-yeh)
From the French patois meaning "to fool around".
Jocelyn, me eh have no time to chicanier wit' all yuh in de Mall nuh!

chic chic
The tiny air pockets made from blowing into pieces of balloon latex. Children love to hear the squeaking noises when they are rubbed.
Careful yuh doh swallow dem chic chic yuh playin' wit' eh Robin.

chikee chong (chee-kee-chong)
A paper kite with long tail.
Why yuh mash up mih chikee chong for?

chicken chest (chik-en ches)
A small chest frame; usual refers to a puny male with narrow chest bone.
Move yuh chicken chest self from near mih boy an' let mih pass.

chikeepek(s)
It means a small person or child. It can be used in the singular or plural form.
What a cute little chikeepek daughter yuh have dere!

chilibibi (chee-lee-bee-bee)
A candy made of sugar and grated roast corn. It is sold in cone-shaped packets.
Remember de good ole days when we children used to buy chilibibi outside de school?

Chinee coconut (chi-nee co-ca nut)
A variety of short coconut palm with golden nuts and sweet water.
When ah tell yuh ah miss mih Chinee coconut tree ah plant in de yard.

Chinee creole (chi-nee cree-ole) (*see* harquai)
A person of mixed races that are Chinese and African. It may be said the other way around.
Oh gorm! Mr. Lam Poon dead? He was a nice Chinee creole man.

Chinee food (chi-nee food)
The Trinidadian Chinese food that is tasty with local seasonings.
I went China an' it eh have no food dere better dan we Chinee food!

Chinee laundry (chi-nee laun-dree)
A place where you get your clothes dry-cleaned. It used to be the name also of a local music band.
We used to follow Chinee Laundry an dem anywhere dey was playing at a fete.

Chinee tamarind (chi-nee tam-bran)
The same as "tambran dasan", a small brown fruit with acid seeds. You have to roll and soften it before eating.
Ah see dey sellin' Chinee tamarind in de grocery now!

chinksin' (chink-sin)
To hold back one's hand in a game or to back squeeze when unwilling to pay up.
Stop chinksin' an' put yuh money where yuh mout is!

chinky (chink-ee)
Very small; tiny or diminutive.
We used to peep out through de chinky key hole to watch Mammy an' Pappy quarrellin'.

chip
To chip is what you do on Carnival Tuesday night. They are the short tired steps trying to keep in time with the road march.
Ah so tired ah coulda hardly chip down de road to catch up wit' all yuh.

chip chip
An edible bi-valved shell-fish found at low tide on the beach especially in Manzanilla and Mayaro; good in curry, soup or souse.
Mih favourite appetizer is chip chip in shado beni at mih mother in law's parties.

chirrup chirrup (*see*** diré diré)**

choka (choke-ah)
Cooked leaves and/or vegetables, East Indian style. It is extremely spicy.
Mih neighbour baigan choka smellin' real good. An' she makin' sada roti to go wit' it!

chokey (cho-kee)
A tight-fitting space; too close for comfort; huddled together.
If yuh see de chokey place he rentin' jes to say he livin' in posh area!

choo koo loonks
A term of endearment often used for a plump female child or person; an intimate word for your darling or sweetheart.
Mable, yuh will forever be my darlin' choo koo loonks!

Choo you! / Choo dat!
It could have come from the Chinese *Qu ni de* meaning "Go away!" or "Damn!" *Qu*, pronounced "choo", while *ni* means "you".
Me eh want to tell you "choo you" because it eh a nice ting to say.

chook (chuk)
A puncture in the flesh, usually caused by a sharp object.
De man foot get chook when he jump on de floor board nail!

chookoo fleet
A local word used to ridicule something small and insignificant.
Is dat chookoo fleet piece ah property dem want to sell for so much!

choonks
A term of endearment for a plump male or female partner.
Come here choonks leh meh give yuh a hug up.

choo poule
An exclamation of dismissal. It originally meant "go away fowl".
Choo poule man! Leh Mervyn stay dere an' wait for mih.

chow
Any fruit or vegetable pickle made with lots of salt and hot pepper;
green mango is the best choice for making a chow.
Dat rose mango tree just waitin' for we to make a good mango chow.

chow chow
An imported mustard pickle popular at Christmas time that goes with
baked ham and pastelles. Now bottled locally.
Dey doh make chow chow like dey used to make in de past!

chow mien (chow min)
Cantonese-styled noodles now adapted into a creolized dish of stir-
fried vegetables with or without shredded meat.
Dis Chinee chow mien tastin' like reel Trini food boy!

chow har luk (chow ha look)
A Trinidadian version of a Cantonese shrimp dish in tomato sauce.
*When Niki ordered a plate a chow har luk in London all dem people
surprise she could talk Chinee!*

chowkie (chow-kee)
A breadboard used for rolling dough.
Pass meh de chowkie nah Betaa.

Christmas ham
This brings back memories of the salty imported ham encased in a tar jacket. It was subsequently boiled in an oil tin on an outside fire at Christmas time.
Boy ah have only to tink 'bout long time Christmas ham an' mih mout does water!

chuckouter (chuk-outta)
A person delegated to move someone forcefully out of a fete.
Where yuh goin' wit' dat body? Yuh lookin' like a chuckouter!

chunkay (choon-kay)
The act of pouring oil in a pot in which a piece of garlic had been burnt.
Girlzie, leh mih teach yuh how to chunkay de pot.

chupidee (choo-pid-ee)
A very daft person.
Dah boy so chupidee he let he cousin take all he marbles.

chupidness (choo-pid-nis)
Gross stupidity; nonsense.
Is Keith Smith who say is only chupidness coulda make we Strike Squad lose dat World Cup!

churria (choo-ree-ah)
Thick East Indian bracelets of gold or silver worn in pairs.
Ah had two precious churria from mih grandmother dat a bandit tief off mih hand.

chutney
East Indian sweet and hotly spiced pickle. Now used to describe East Indian singing influenced by the calypso or soca beat.
Drupatee use to be boss in chutney singin' competition.

chutney soca
A musical adaptation of East Indian and African rhythms that is an indigenous musical art form.
Hey! Now Rikki Jai is master at de chutney soca competition each year.

Chuts man!
An exclamation of aggravation; used to express annoyance or irritation:
Chuts man! Go 'way Mosquito, yuh find mih blood sweet or what!

clean neck fowl
A common breed of backyard chicken.
Is dat clean neck fowl self de neighbour try to tief.

closet
A latrine in the countryside; also called a WC.
Yuh fadder build a closet wit' a window so he coulda watch out from?

coal pot
A West Indian iron pot still used for cooking in country districts.
Yuh eh know 'bout dem days when Granny an' dem use a coal pot for cookin' an' ironin'?

coal pot dougla
A curly head of hair sraightened with Vaseline and an iron comb, that is electric or heated over a fire.
Before relaxer cream come in it was coal pot dougla for so in town.

cobweb broom
A special cleaning tool made of coconut fibre used for removing spider webs.
Ah go fix up dem spider webs with a good cobweb broom from de market.

cocobay
Physical deformity left by leprosy; used to describe a scarred body.
Ah did warn she to stop tellin' dat story 'bout she cocobay grandfadder.

cocoa butter
The fat extracted from the cocoa bean, used for removing pigment spots on skin.
Leh mih put some cocoa butter on dat black spot yuh have on yuh leg.

cockset
A brand of mosquito coil designed to ward off mosquitoes and night insects with its powerful fumes.
Ah hope yuh buy enough cockset for de weekend down Mayaro!

cocksure
Overly confident; strutting around with an attitude.
If yuh see how dem new Ministers struttin' around like dem cocksure 'bout de nex five years!

cock up yuh foot
To sit with one foot over the other or to put up both legs.
Natasha, it eh lady-like to cockup yuh foot so!

cocoa tea
A thick oily chocolate drink made from dried and grated cocoa beans and flavoured with spices like cinnamon and tonka bean.
Drink up yuh cocoa tea before it get cold.

cocoa 'pagnol (ko-ko pai-yol)
From the patois *cocoa espagnol*. A racial mixture of Carib, Spanish and African bloods. It originates from the peasant class on the cocoa estates and valleys of Venezuela.
She lookin' jes like mih cocoa 'pagnol cousin Josefina Lopez from Tamana.

cocoa suer (ko-ko sway)
From the French patois meaning "sweat of the cocoa", it describes a strong masculine body odour.
He jes done wuk outside so yuh could imagine how he smellin' of cocoa suer.

coconut
A tropical palm tree; it can also refer to the shape of one's head.
Nello, move yuh coconut so ah could see where ah drivin'.

coconut cart
A method of transport by oxen or donkey and once popular with coconut vendors around the Savannah.
If yuh see de fancy ting round de Savannah! Like coconut cart is history now eh boy!

coconut drop
A muffin made with sugar and grated coconut dropped in blobs on a
tin and baked.
Ah used to like to buy coconut drop from Mr. Cheemooke bakery.

cocorite (ko-ko-reet)
A small palm fruit. Also the name of a place on the seafront to the
west of Port of Spain.
Is ah long time since ah eat cocorite from de estate up in Lopinot.

cocoyea (ko-kee-ay)
The veins from coconut leaves. When stripped and dried they are
bunched together to make a broom or used singly for making kites.
Harry, hurry up an' make de cocoyea broom for mih nuh!

cocrico (kok-ree-ko)
National bird of Tobago but often considered a pest by farmers.
Dem cocrico so miserable ah cyar believe it on we Coat of Arms.

cog
To copy or sneak a look into somebody else's copybook.
Anil doh cog from mih book or ah go tell Teach.

cokee eye
Used to tease someone with crossed eyes or who squints.
Doh mind she cokee eye she could see better dan you.

cokeeoko (ko-kee-o-ko)
Carrying someone usually a child on one's back.
*De fadder was givin' he son a cokeeoko up de hill when both ah
dem fall down.*

cold like dog nose
A reference to the coldness of a dog's nose.
De microwave eh wukkin' so de food cold like dog nose.

come go
It could become "come leh we go", meaning "let us go."
Come go leh we find de cricket bat an' hit some ball.

comesse (kom-mes) (*see* **cuchur**)
A patois word meaning "confusion"; indulging in intrigue.
We people cyar solve nutten as we does live from one comesse to de nex.

comme ci comme ça (com see com sa)
A patois reply to "How are you doing today?" It means "just so so".
Me? Ah comme ci comme ça today an' so what 'bout you?

common
To denote vulgarity.
Miss Lady daughter was gettin' on too common in de party.

compère (kom-peh)
Of French origin, it means "godfather".
Compère come here an' sit down by yuh godchile.

conch
A large univalve shellfish found in rocky coastal areas; it is a popular native dish in Tobago.
Me cyar wait to taste Tantie Ollie conch soup up in Speyside.

confuffle (kon-fuf-ful)
A state of confusing or of being confused.
Doh confuffle mih brains wit' yuh talk 'bout a little raise now!

Congo
A word made popular with Sparrow's calypso about the Congo man in Africa.
Yuh come like Sparrow or what? Imagine he say he never eat a white meat yet in he song 'bout de Congo man!

Congo barra
Used for any obeah man delving into the occult; associated with stick-fighting.
Few nowadays know 'bout de stick-fighting chant: "mettez lumière by Congo barra".

congoree (kong-o-ree)
A millipede common in gardens, quite harmless but feared.
Doh harm de congoree. Yuh eh know dem good for de garden.

congosa (kong-o-sah)
A wild type of behaviour; immodest dressing.
She behavin' too congosa for mih to take she on.

congotay (kong-o-tay)
Usually introduced by the words "one day, one day, congotay", it gives warning about an unpleasant eventuality.
De boy followin' bad company so ah tell he one day, one day congotay.

conk out
To pass out from tiredness or drink.
Ah bong to conk out soon as ah reach home from all dis traffic jam.

constackle (kon-stak-ul)
To attack another playfully or aggressively; to grab by the scruff of the neck.
Me eh do he nutten but de man constackle mih jes so.

contact
To have a relationship with someone who helps cut the red tape to make life easier.
Well give meh yuh contact in de Licensin' office.

cooboose (koo-boos)
A hole-in-the-wall; cramped living quarters; a derogatory way to describe a home. Origin possibly from "coop" or "cooped up".
If yuh see de little cooboose whey dem was livin' in!

coo coo
A Caribbean staple made of boiled corn meal and ladled into a pot with seasonings, ochroes, and butter. It is great with steamed fish and lots of lime dressing.
Nick, whey yuh expect mih to find ting to make coo coo an' saltfsh in dis cold place behind God back in Canada!

cookup
A pot of food that has leftover to make a casserole-styled dish; the combining of several food items to make a stew or pelau.
Ah eh fussin' for lunch today; is a cookup ah makin'.

coolin'
Any brew that cleans out, cools and refreshes the body.
Is ah good coolin' yuh need wit' plenty watercress to clean out yuh body.

cool so
It means "just so"; sometimes "level so" or "dry so"; something that has happened out of the ordinary.
Cool so de man come an' take 'way he chile from mih for de weekend.

cool yuhself
A warning to avoid getting worked up over an issue; stay calm.
Cool yuhself mih boy or yuh go dead from heart attack.

copecetic (ko-pa-seh-tik)
A word that means looking and acting sharp.
Yuh lookin' copectic fuh yuh first day out to work!

coquette (koh-ket)
From the French *coqueter,* "to flirt". A look that is demure and lady-like; shy.
Look at de coquette dressed up in she Sunday best!

corbeau (ko-bo)
A French word meaning "crow" or "raven". These scavenger birds proliferate in garbage dumps and feast on refuse.
Dem vagrant jes like corbeau so leh we help dem nah!

Corbeau Town (ko-bo tong)
The area west of the Red House around Richmond and Sackville streets, where sea and swamp met originally.
Is mih family what develop Corbeau Town in dem early days.

corn husk
What remains after eating the corn; the corn cob.
All yuh eat de corn an' lef de corn husk dey on de ground!

coscorob
A fresh water fish.
How much dem coscorob sellin' for today?

cosquelle (kos-kel)
A patois word meaning "overdressed". Used to describe someone dressed up in loud and wild fashion; ridiculously garbed.
De woman feel she dress up nice but she lookin' cosquelle.

cote ci cote la (ko-tay-see ko-tay-la)
A patois word meaning "a little bit of this and a little bit of that". It is also the title of John Mendes' popular version of the vernacular.
She fill meh up wit' a little cote ci cote la 'bout de state of de country an' she family an' ting.

country bookie
Used to describe someone who comes to town from the country.
Mih half-brudder come to tong dress up like a real country bookie in plaid pants.

cousin mahoe (koo-zeh ma-hoe)
Of patois origin.A medicinal bark popular for making teas for flu and internal disorders.
Tantie send some cousin mahoe for Pappy who cyar pass water.

couverte pocham (koo-vay-tee po-sham)
An overnight toilet with a lid.
Dat hat yuh wearin' lookin' more like dem long time couverte pocham!

cover lead
Originates from the English "coverlet" or bed cover; bed sheets or linens.
Yuh go an' rumffle up de good cover lead ah make up de bed wit'!

cowheel soup
A soup made from cow's heel and boiled to a soft jelly with dumplings and provisions.
Dey sellin' cowheel soup all over de place nowadays.

cow-itch
A plant that has the same irritating effect as stinging nettle; it describes a state of restlessness.
Why yuh cyar keep yuh tail quiet? Like yuh have cow-itch or what!

coz
From the word "cousin"; anyone you wish to address affectionately.
*Come nuh coz an' open de door for yuh pardner who come lookin'
for yuh!*

crab back
The shell of the crab that is cleaned and stuffed with spiced crab meat
and breadcrumbs and then baked.
*What yuh havin' fuh appetizer? Crab back? Oh gorm me cyar wait
fuh dat!*

crab race
A sport in Tobago with crabs taking part in competition.
Is since when yuh taken up wit' crab race in Tobago?

craf
Originated from "craft" meaning a work of art, which describes a
nice-looking woman.
She used to be one nice-lookin' craf when she was young!

crapaud (kra-po)
The French word for "toad"; used in "crapaud smoke yuh pipe",
meaning "watch out for the inevitable bad luck".
*If we go on wit' all dis greed an ting, watch out! Crapaud smoke we
pipe!*

crapaud foot writin' (kra-po-foot writin')
Illegible scrawl or script; bad penmanship.
*Nobody could make out yuh crapaud foot writin'. Like yuh is ah
doctor or what!*

cravat
A piece of male necktie attire; also the name of a bird indigenous to
Trinidad known as Trinidad Euphonia. Its scientific name is *Euphonia
trinitatis.*
Like ah hearin' ah cravat singin' chee chee.

crazow (kray-zow)
A crazy person; scatter-brained; acting irresponsibly.
*Is mih crazow nephew dat turn calypsonian an' call heself "De
Mighty Crazy".*

Creole
From the Spanish *criollo,* a native born person regardless of ethnic origin. French Creole still refers to native born children of Europeans in particular of French immigrants.
Is de Creole in he wha make Tony turn kaisonian.

creolize
To hybridize. In Trini parlance it means mixed with African blood.
Ask dem French creole who bring half of Africa to creolize de West Indies?

crepesole (krep-sole)
A canvas shoe with ribbed rubber sole; forerunner to sneakers.
Granny does call mih good Reebok a crepesole!

crick crack
A popular West Indian ending to a local folk tale. It is usually followed by "monkey break he back".
Merle Hodge also write a book wit' de title Crick Crack?

Croisée (kway-zay)
From the French word meaning "crossing", it is a popular junction on the Eastern Main Road in the town of San Juan.
Doh forget to meet meh down by de Croisée.

cross(es)
Any trouble, usually coming in the form of a person. Often used in the plural as an exclamation of despair.
Well look at mih crosses! Yuh mean ah have to face dis cross again!

crochety (kro-sheh-tee)
Fussy; used to describe a quarrelsome old woman; someone who is disagreeable.
Lord! Ah hope ah doh end up ah crochety ole maid like Nen Nen.

cry cry baby
Someone who acts immaturely; a person who frets constantly and complains.
Stop getting' on like a cry cry baby an' grow up nuh.

cuatro (kwa-tro)
From the Spanish *cuatro,* meaning "four", it is a four-stringed musical instrument introduced by the settlers from South America. It is popular in parang bands at Christmas time.
Dis cuatro come from Venezuela since mih grandfadder days.

cucheela (koo-chee-la)
An East Indian spicy chutney made of grated green mango and mustard oil. It is also spelt "kucheela".
Tantie Merle ask mih to bring some cucheela dat Lakshmi make for she.

cuchur (coo-choor/kuchur)
A Hindi word meaning "confusion and intrigue"; similar to *comesse* or *bachannal.*
Me eh want to get mix up in dah political cuchur in all yuh bloggin'.

cuff down (kuff dong)
To administer a blow so as to throw the other off balance; to knock down a person.
If yuh see how he try to cuff down he own pardner!

cunumunu (koo-noo-moo-noo)
A stupid person; someone who does not understand what is going on.
She so bright, so how come she marry dat cunumunu!

currant roll (co-rants-roll)
A traditional flaky pastry with abundant currants embedded between its layers; a national favourite.
Yuh does pass by Linda's jes so yuh could pick up all dem currant roll?

curry
A combination of herbs and spices that are ground into a powder and used when cooking East Indian style.
It eh have nutten to beat a curry duck an' a good river lime.

cush cush
A root tuber with soft starchy interior when cooked, it comes in white or purple varieties; and it is a substitute for potato.
Christmas in Arima is good cush cush an' stew chicken.

cushy
A comfortable position.
All she children have cushy job in de Civil Service so she doh have to worry 'bout a ting.

cuss
To curse. It may be used to "to cuss up" or "to cuss down".
Boy show some respect an' doh cuss she up so nah!

cuss bud
Someone who enjoys using obscene language. It originates from birds like the parrot or macaw that were taught to swear.
Doh worry to tell meh 'bout dat cuss bud friend of yours because me eh like she at all!

cut ass
To administer blows causing physical and emotional damage to another.
Long time parents woulda give all yuh children a severe cut ass to make all yuh behave.

cut eye
The disparaging look given with a deliberate closing of the eye and turning away from the offender.
Ah give she one cut eye when she finally bring back mih book.

cutlass
The razor sharp instrument used for cutting bush or sugar cane.
Known also as a *machete* or *gilpin*.
Careful yuh doh cut yuhself wit' dat cutlass!

cut Lent
The act of bending the little finger with a friend in an attempt to keep
the promise to abstain from something like candy during the period of
Lent.
Come leh we cut Lent not to smoke nah boy.

cut tail (*see* **cut ass**)

cut up
To be angry or disturbed over something or someone; irritable and
fretful.
*Is yuh who have meh so cut up since yuh gorn an' mash up mih
bike.*

cut yuh nature
To lessen one's libido by eating something too acid or salty.
*Ah tired tellin' yuh dat eating too much sour cherry go cut yuh
nature.*

cuyenade (koo-yeh-narde)
A patois word meaning "foolishness"; nonsense.
Stop talkin' so much cuyenade before ah tell yuh wife on yuh.

cuyoh (koo-yoh)
Acting stupidly; unable to think clearly; allowing oneself to be fooled.
*Gyul behave yuhself an' stop actin' so cuyoh over de Guyanese
man!*

cyar see yuh for love nor money
Used to stress the difficulty one has in connecting with another.
Ay! Ay! Wha goin' on? Me cyar see yuh for love nor money!

D

da da head
Used to describe uncombed or matted Afro hair; usually associated with vagrants.
Dah eh no Afro hairstyle dat is plain da da head.

Dame Lorraine (dam loh-rane)
An old time female Carnival character overdressed and played by a male.
He did like to dress up in woman like Dame Lorraine too bad!

dancin' cocoa
Originates from the art of trampling on the cocoa beans while they are drying in the sun so as to remove the outer covering and make them smooth and shiny.
How yuh movin' so? Like you dancin' cocoa or what?

dancin' mih
To avoid coming to the point; to deliberately mislead; to bramble or evade a question.
Stop dancin' mih an' takin' me to Little Englan' an' tell me de truth.

dan dan
A frock or nice-looking outfit.
Who give yuh dat nice dan dan for Christmas?

dasheen
A popular ground provision and staple. Considered "blue food" by Trinidadians. Originally introduced by the Chinese, one theory is that it comes from the French who referred to it as *de la Chine.*
Wha kinda dasheen yuh buy dey for mih in de market!

dasheen bush
Leaves and stems of dasheen used for making *callaloo*.
Pick de young green dasheen bush for de callaloo.

dat beat all cockfight
Used to describe the ultimate in a situation.
De way ah see all yuh make up dat beat all cockfight.

dat eh come
To try but to fail.
Dat eh come! Yuh jes like yuh fadder wit' he stale jokes!

dat good for yuh
To serve one right; one deserves what one gets.
Dat good for yuh! Yuh shouldn't put yuh hand in de stingin' nettle.

Dat is you?
Is that you?
Dat is you? Ah cyar make yuh out at all in de night.

deadin' (ded-in)
Used often with the words "with laughter" to describe an extreme state or condition.
Euls gyul yuh have mih deadin' with laughter on de phone.

dead out
Dead beat; tired to the point of passing out; any object that looks old and beaten up.
Whey yuh see me here, ah good dead out after playin' football wit' Simon.

dealin'
The act of playing a hand in cards; or the act of indulging in the occult; or the act of trading in drugs.
It have plenty people who dealin' in drug an' who have we country in trouble.

decked off/out
To dress up and strut around; dressed to kill.
Like yuh decked off to impress de chick!

dee ray dee ray
A little bit of something; a handful; going half and half; possibly from the French *dire*, "to say".
Go dee ray dee ray on de macaroni pie as ah is on a diet.

dem say (*see*** town say)**

depuis (dey-pwee)
From the French *depuis*, meaning "since". In patois d*epuis ki temps* means "since when".
Depuis ki temps yuh does remember to come an' say good morning?

deputy
An outside woman or man, made popular by Calypsonian Penguin's 1982 calypso "A deputy essential".
A deputy is a fact of life for many Trini men.

devil
A sexy-looking woman.
If yuh see de devil rollin' she rear end as she pass mih!

Devil's Woodyard
A mud volcano, a popular attraction in south Trinidad.
De geography class goin' on a visit to Devil's Woodyard.

DEWD (dood)
The acronym for the Development and Environmental Works Divison initated by the People's National Movement; a state of laissez-faire.
Me eh like some ah dem DEWD workers! Ah is a good righteous hardwukkin' breadwinner.

dew fallin'
The approach of dusk or dawn when the air becomes cooler.
Andy mudder tell him to put on he cap as dew fallin' an' he could catch cold.

deya (dee-ya)
The small clay container used for "lighting up' ceremony at the Hindu festival of Divali.
Come leh we start fixin' up de bamboo frame to hold de deya for tomorrow lightin' up.

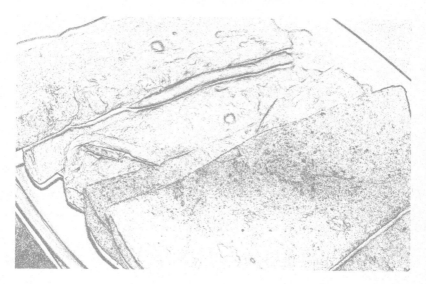

dey dey
A childish way to say "goodbye".
Tell Mammie dey dey an' stay a good gyul okay?

dhal (da-a-l)
A Hindi word for split peas, a staple of East Indian cuisine. In north India it is known as *matar ki daal*.
Indrani, it too early to grind de dahl for de roti.

dhalpuri (dal-poo-ree)
A thin dough filled with ground *dhal* and wrapped around spicy curried meats or veggies. *Puri* is a small pancake in India.
Ah could'na wait to get back home to eat de real dhalpuri dat Adelsia does make.

dholak (doe-lak)
A two-sided East Indian drum used at weddings and special occasions.
Ah jes did love to hear dem drummers beat de dholak.

dhoti (doe-tee)
The loin cloth worn by East Indian males in the past and still popular as ceremonial garb.
Come an' see how nice Boyzie lookin' in he dhoti an' ting.

diable diable (*see* **jab jab**)

dig
To take note of or to assess a position; to check out a situation.
Dig de haircut nuh. It jes like a Mohawk in dem Westerns.

dig out mih eye
To take advantage of a situation.
Every day yuh want something. Like yuh want to dig out mih eye!

digs out
To make a hasty departure.
Leh me digs outta here before yuh old man return an' catch meh in he house.

Dimanche Gras
The lavish Sunday night show that precedes the two days of Carnival street revelry, literally means "Big Sunday" in French.
We goin' to de Savannah as usual for Dimanche Gras.

dingolay (deen-go-lay)
Of French patois origin meaning "to collapse"; to fall or tumble down usually in dance. It can also mean to dither or fool around.
De sweet music make everybody feel to dingolay like mad.

diré diré (dee-ray dee-ray)
From the French *dire,* "to say", but it has come to mean a little at a time. It can mean 'I will tell you when to stop." *Chirrup chirrup* has the same meaning.
Go diré diré wit' puttin' all dat food on mih plate.

dish up
To pass out or serve up something such as food, clothes or money.
Yuh better dish up de blue note before dey throw yuh tail in jail.

ditay payee (dee-tay pay-ee)
A patois word for a shrub used in making tea for curing fever. The morning dew collected from the leaves is used as an eye wash.
Go an' pick some ditay payee for yuh grandmother nah!

Divali (dee-wah-lee)
The Hindu festival of lights.
Ah goin' an' take de children for a drive to see de lightin' up for Divali in Aranguez.

do for
To get even with somebody.
Watch out! She tief mih bangle but ah go do for she!

dogs dead
All is lost; in trouble.
Oh Gawd! Teacher find out ah break biche now mih dogs dead.

doh
A contraction of "do not" or "don't", it is used in places like "doh make joke" which is an exclamation of surprise.
Doh make joke! Chester really comin' for Carnival?

doh care
Someone who is irresponsible.
Me eh able wit' she doh care attitude at all.

doh dig nutten
Don't worry.
Doh dig nutten. Is he Mr. Fix-it self who go straighten out yuh car.

doh eat nice
A description of seriousness; one who does not brook nonsense.
Doh complain 'bout yuh salary as de bossman doh eat nice at all.

doh feel no how
One must not worry.
Doh feel no how ah go fix up yuh toilet seat fuh yuh.

doh fool yuh fat
Stop fooling yourself.
Doh fool yuh fat as she have every intention to marry de man.

Doh mind dat!
Don't be afraid; don't take it seriously.
Wipe yuh eye an' stop crying. Doh mind dat! De boy beg pardon.

Doh skylark!
Stop fooling around and get serious.
When I take up dis ruler, doh make skylark wit' yuh Homework eh!

Doh try dat!
One must not think deception will work.
Him is yuh cousin Peter? Doh try dat! I too long down here.

dong de islands
The picturesque islands located off the north-western tip of Trinidad, Gasparee and Monos being the more popular vacation spots.
It was dong de islands where mih Mom and Dad spend their honeymoon in de fifties.

dong de road
To travel an indefinite distance.
Ah comin' back jes now. Ah goin' dong de road to come back.

donkey eye
A large round seed like a donkey's eye. Children love to rub it against the concrete to make it hot.
Mammy, she come an' burn me with de hot donkey eye she rub up on de concrete.

donkeys years
Colloquial for "it's been a long time since…"
Ashram boy, me eh see yuh in donkeys years! Whey yuh wuz?

doods
A derivative of *doux doux* from the patois meaning 'sweetie'; an expression of endearment.
How yuh goin' dis morning doods?

doolaha
A Hindi word for bridegroom.
Come an' see how nice de doolaha lookin'.

doolahin
A Hindi word for bride.
Vishnu goin' by he doolahin house wit' he family.

dort dort (doe doe)
From the patois word *dormer,* "to sleep", a lullaby that puts babies to
sleep
*"Dort dort petit popo..." is what ah remember mih Grannie used to
sing to put we to sleep.*

do so
Followed by "eh like so", it means that seeking revenge may not be
such a good idea.
*Do so eh like so is what all yuh people mus' remember when de
table turn.*

dotish
Stupid; someone who is easily fooled. A derogatory word from the
English "doltish".
*Little boy learn yuh lesson an' doh come out dotish like yuh big
brudder.*

dou dou (doo-doo)
From the French word *doux/douce,* meaning "sweet" or "sweetness";
a term of endearment when calling out to pretty women.
Come an' sit nex to me dou dou darling.

dou dou darl
An endearment from the patois meaning "sweet little darling".
*Yuh will always be my dou dou darl so come here fuh meh to give
yuh a big hug up.*

doubles
Two lightly fried pieces of dough with spicy curried *channa* (chick
peas) filling between; a popular roadside or breakfast snack.
*Is doubles for mih breakfast dis morning chase down by a good
coconut water.*

douen (dwen)
A folklore character said to be the spirit of an unbaptised child who
roams the forest. His form is that of a naked child about two to three
feet in height, with face hidden behind a large conical straw hat. His
feet are turned backward to fool the unwary.
Is to see how Alfred Codallo painted dem douen picture.

dougla (doug-lah)
A mix of African and East Indian. It originates from *doogala* which is
a Hindi word.
Dat couple make one nice dougla chile!

Down de Main
Across the Gulf of Paria on the South Amrican Mainland.
*Dem fishermen have it to do wit' de traffikin' an' ting from Down
de Main.*

downs (dongs)
A small acid fruit with a hard seed in crunchy white flesh. Proper
spelling is "doncs" but for some unknown reason the natives call it
"downs".
*Me an' mih cousins used to go down by de sea in Woodbrook where
it did have plenty downs trees.*

down town (dong tong)
The Main Drag that is Frederick Street and its immediate environs in
Port of Spain.
Oh Gorm! Down town Port of Spain eh nutten like it used to be!

Drag Brothers
Young craftsmen of African descent who took over Independence
Square opposite Bankers' Row in the seventies.
Ah used to go down by de Drag Brothers to fix mih leather shoes.

draw ah chair
To pull a chair.
Draw ah chair an' come talk to me as mih ears eh so good.

dread / dread locks
An African hairstyle grown long and uncombed.
Is to see how de middle class boys gorn dread now!

dress down
Move down to make space for someone. *Dresser* in French means to
straighten out or fix.
*Mih big fat Tantie in Church always want me to dress down for she
to sit.*

dress to kill / dress up
Decked off in fancy wear to impress; over dressed.
Now he get a little wuk he does dress to kill when he goin' to lime.

drevait (dree-vay)
To wander around in search of a good lime; to hang around.
De gyul cyar keep she tail quiet. She like to drevait too bad.

Driver, ah go take it here
A colourful way to ask the person at the steering wheel to let one get off at that point; commonly used with taxi drivers.
Not so fast Mr. Driver, ah go take it here.

drop(s)
A "stop" or a "ride" in the singular form, but it could mean a "coconut cake" in the plural form.
Ah go take a drop down de road by cousin Clementina. Is she wha does make some nice coconut drops.

drop off
To stop the vehicle and let someone out.
Doh forget ah go drop off near Charlie rumshop.

dropsy
A state of sleepiness; drowsiness.
Is dat fete last night wha have yuh lookin' like yuh have dropsy.

drouette (dwi-yet)
From the French word for a particular style of dress that Martiniquan women wear, it is adapted as their national costume, which is made of plaid fabric with full skirt tucked up at the side with lacy petticoat.
Is de beautiful drouette wha make she de Carnival Queen.

drumology
The art of drum-beating.
Ay! Like yuh went University to study dat drumology.

drunken sailor
An old time taunt to poke fun at someone with a staggering gait; a form of sailor mas.
Every year Mannie did like to play drunken sailor too bad!

drunk or sober
Followed by "mind yuh business", it warns of keeping your focus on things without being distracted.
When tings getting' hectic drunk or sober is to mind yuh business.

Dry River
The mile long paved bed of the St Ann's River in east Port of Spain and its environs.
It eh today ah livin' in Dry River so dat is how come ah know all ah town business.

dry so
A state of suddeness; an unexpected turn of events.
Dry so yuh stop talkin' to mih?

dry wedder
Used with reference to cars that seem to work only when the weather is fine or to a person who recognizes you only when convenient.
Dis is a real dry wedder car. It sometime-ish jes like yuh friend who only know yuh when you on top.

duck
Zero. "To duck out" means to get out from a tight spot. It can also mean "to bend down".
Duck yuh head so yuh could squeeze under de fence.

duncey head
A slow learner.
Yuh eh want to be no duncey head little girl so leh mih teach you de alphabet.

duttiness
To curse; the ultimate in vulgar behaviour or conversation.
He like too much duttiness fuh me so is to leave he right dere.

E

early o'clock
The earliest time possible; anytime earlier than expected.
Is early o'clock ah straighten out de Mister on what is mine an'
what is he own.

ease up
To let up on something; to go slowly or gently.
Is to ease up on de pedal or else yuh go mash up de gearbox.

ease up de tension
To let up on the pressure.
Stop worryin' 'bout de family an' ease up on de tension. Everyting
go wuk out.

East Indian Arrival Day
Celebrated in May to mark the arrival of the first boatload of
indentured Indians on the Fatel Rozack in 1845.
De celebrations for East Indian Arrival Day will blow yuh mind.

easy like kissin' hand
Describes the simplicity of an action.
Fixin' dis ole washing machine come easy like kissin' hand.

eat ah food
A dehumanizing reference to the need to eat to live.
Yuh eh know some man mus' tief to eat ah food!

eat de bread
"To eat de bread de devil knead" describes the state of having a hard
time surviving.
If yuh play de fool an' lorse dat work all ah we go eat de bread de
devil knead.

eating nice
Used in the negative to denote an unpleasant attitude.
Me eh eatin' nice at all today so yuh better watch yuhself!

eat me out
To devour everything.
Buh if yuh go on like dat you go eat me out of house an' land!

eat parrot bottom
A talkative person.
Nairoon cyar stop talking, is like he eat parrot bottom.

eddoes
A variety of ground provision or root tuber, which is a staple.
How come dem eddoes so small?

Eh bien oui donc donc!
An exclamation to describe a state of surprise. From the French patois meaning "Okay" or "Well all right then!"
we used to call Mr. Ramon Fortune "Eh bien oui donc donc!".

Eh?
A question; or to look for affirmation.
Eh? Wha yuh say yuh comin' with me?

Eh eh!
A negative exclamation to emphasise the point being made. Simply put it means "no".
Eh eh! Ah eh goin' no way wit' you.

Eh heh!
An affirmation or an exclamation of dismay.
Eh heh! Ah ketch yuh eatin' mih chicken foot.

eh makin' joke
No nonsense will be tolerated.
Stop ticklin' me! I eh makin' no joke!

eh no true member
Not honest about something or someone; not a team player; unreliable.
Doh worry to include she in de lime. She eh no true member.

Eid ul fitr (eed-ool-fiteer)
The Muslim festival of thanksgiving; a National holiday after the new moon is sighted during the holy month of Ramadan.
Yuh must come an' eat by we for de Eid ul Fitr.

Emancipation Day
A National holiday celebrated on August 1, to pay tribute to those who fought for emancipation of African slaves.
Dey have band an' ting paradin' on Emancipation Day in Port of Spain.

empty bag cyar stand
To describe the lack of effort from someone who is suffering from hunger.
Is time to break for lunch because remember empty bag cyar stand!

endless
Never-ending.
Doh let she fool yuh. She family have endless bread.

end up
To find oneself in a questionable situation.
Go on shoppin' like dat an' yuh go end up in de poor house.

Ent?
Isn't that so?
Ent? I have good teet jes like Mammy own?

entremetia (en-treh-meh-tee-ah)
From Spanish *entremeter,* "to meddle" or "to interfere", it refers to someone who is pushy and meddlesome.
De mother spoil she so she too entremetia fuh mih.

enviggle
From the English word "inveigle", it means to encourage or to involve someone.
Doh try to enviggle mih in yuh comesse!

every man Jack
Everybody without exception.
Ah want every man Jack to get out de dirt an' go under de garden hose.

expectin' a flood
Wearing ill-fitting pants that are way too short.
How yuh pants turn up so, like yuh expectin' ah flood!

explashiate (ex-pla-shee-ate)
A word coined to reflect the loud, showy and ridiculous.
Doh come here an' explashiate about yuh big job dong Sando.

ex tempo
From the Latin *ex tempore,* meaning "out of time", it is a form of Calypso in which the opponents compete and sing spontaneously witty repartees in verse.
Calypsonians Lord Caresser an' de Mighty Short Pants is jes two of de original ex tempo kings.

eye up
To look with favour on something or someone.
If yuh did see how dat man did eye mih up at de wedding!

F

fafoulage
From the French *fafouiller,* meaning "to rummage". Fussy; full of frills and furbelows; extremely decorative; over-dressed.
Ah doh like dis outfit at all, it too full ah fafoulage.

fall out
To end a relationship.
Basdeo fall out wit' Anika since she bounce up wit' Kingsley at de fete last week.

fares
Originates from "to make fares", it refers to the job of a prostitute.
Makin' fares is one of de oldes' professions in de world.

farine (fah-reen)
The powdered flour from parched corn or cassava.
Wha have me strong today is all dat farine porridge mih mother used to feed mih.

farse
Out of place, as in "not minding one's own business"; inquisitive; someone who meddles in other people's affairs.
Doh ask mih mih business. Yuh too farse.

farseness
Out-of-place behaviour as in sexual harassment.
If yuh only bring yuh farseness to mih ah go report yuh to de bossman.

fatigue
Used when making a joke at another's expense.
Stop givin' she fatigue nuh, she doh even know de man!

fat pants
A pair of over-sized trousers.
Doh trow away mih fat pants nuh, it go come back in style.

fat pork
A red fruit with soft white pulp.
It has a lot of fat pork trees in Caura.

fat talk
Empty words; an attempt to impress.
All dat fat talk eh go change meh mind as ah eh goin' nowhere wit' yuh.

fatty boolie
Teasing a plump person.
Come here wit' yuh fatty boolie self leh mih give yuh a hug.

favour
Resemblance to someone.
Leh meh see, yuh really favour yuh fadder side of de family.

fedupsy (fed-up-see)
Disenchanted; bored.
When yuh see ah in dis state of fedupsy is to lef meh alone.

feel ah how (*see* **ah how**)

fensin
Any plant used to make hedges or boundaries between neighbours.
Why yuh go an' cut down de fensin bush?

fête
From the French *fête,* meaning "festival, celebration" or simply "party".
It eh have a Trini who doh like to fête.

fête match
A friendly game of cricket or football.
Ah goin' by Krishna family in Caroni dis Sunday since de fête match playin' close to dem.

fever grass
A sharp-smelling medicinal plant used to make teas for colds and malaria.
Doh go an' cut down mih precious fever grass dat Mama did plant!

fig / green fig
Any member of the banana family but in particular the hard green variety used in *sancoche* and vegetarian souse or salad.
Boil de green fig good as ah makin' souse wit' it today.

fight up
To battle with a person or thing.
Leave meh alone leh meh fight up wit' dis housework.

find (fine)
To hold an opinion. It has nothing to do with locating something or someone.
Ah find he shoulda tell she something before he gorn off with dat other woman.

fine bone
Thin or maigre looking person.
Dis gyul only lookin' fine bone but she strong like a lioness.

fini (fee-nee)
From the French *finir*, "to finish"; it can also describe a handicap.
She fini hand didn't prevent she from holdin' down a good job.

fionay (fee-oh-nay)
From the patois word *fioner*, to ridicule, to taunt.
All dat neighbour good to do is to fionay all day.

fire de wuk
To give up the job or to quit unexpectedly.
Is time fuh yuh to fire de wuk or else it go give yuh a serious breakdown.

fireman dance
The dance steps that accompany the stoking of the ship's engine in a sailor band at Carnival.
If yuh did see how Pappy used to do de fireman dance in de band.

fire one
To toast.
Man, come leh we fire one on de chile head dat jes baptize.

fire rage
Boiling with anger.
She really vex wit' de landlord but he eh takin' on she fire-rage.

five fingers
An acid fruit; also known as *carambola*.
When ah was small ah did love five fingers.

fixin' up
To straighten out a matter or to put things right.
See how he go get ah fixin' up when he tell me dem lies.

flag man/woman
A character who leads the mas band with a flag at Carnival.
Is to see dem flag man an' woman wine down on de Big Stage.

flambeau (flam-bo)
From the French, meaning flame; a form of lighting up at night.
*Ah remember dem nights in Toco in de tent dat light up wit'
flambeau an' ting.*

flannel ball
The traditional tennis ball that is made with rubber and felt.
Toss de flannel ball here so ah could show yuh some real tennis tricks.

flare up
A sudden burst of temper.
Well yuh doh have to flare up like dat to tell mih yuh vex!

fleet ah licks
An unusal amount of spanking.
When dey catch de bandit de people bus one fleet ah licks in he tail.

flim
Film as in Kodak or Fuji. It can refer also to a movie.
It eh have no more flim for camera jes as it eh have no more flim showin' in de drive-in cinema.

flit
A commercial name for an insect repellant. It can also mean the movements of a very busy person.
Bring de flit here so ah could drive dis fly crazy.

flo
Loose; lightly packed; spongy or airy.
Dem people tiefin' we blind when dey pack dem goods flo flo.

float
A Trinidadian dough made with lots of baking powder that floats when deep-fried. Popular with fish or *accra*.
Mih belly longin' for a good accra an' float.

floora (flo-ra)
From the word "floor", it refers to a place where a person spends the night when there is no bed available.
Well boy, it look like is floora tonight as Ma cousins comin' to visit.

flour bag sailor
There was a time when sailor costumes were made from the sacking of imported flour.
De onliest big mas he ever play was longtime flour bag sailor!

fob(s)
The small pocket in jacket or pants which the dandy used for his watch or small change or handkerchief.
Take yuh hand out mih fob pocket nuh gyul!

follow fashion
To copy someone else's style. In the old days it used to be accompanied by "chook monkey dog" when used as a taunt.
Come up wit' yuh own ideas nuh gyul an' stop de follow fashion.

food carrier
The triple-decked enamel container that women used to put food for their working men in the good old days.
Mammie! Today we have take-out we eh need no more food carrier!

footie (foo-tee)
An exclamation; a threat that warns of impending disaster; describes a state of futility.
Yuh tink yuh smart but yuh go footie catch yuh tail to eat ah food.

force ripe
As with fruit the same with people; maturing ahead of time; a precocious state.
Doh go an' sell meh any force ripe fig dere nuh!

for days
An indefinite time frame; a state of amazement.
Oh Gawd! When ah tell yuh, dah man used to be handsome for days!

foreday morning (fo-day mornin')
The period just before day break.
Come foreday morning we go meet by Blanchisseuse ole road.

for so (fuh so)
An exclamation of surprise to denote "much" or "a lot of".
Dis mango ripe for so!

frankomen
A way to say "honest-to-goodness" or "frankly speaking".
Frankomen is to leave dis blight place an' start all over again.

fraquitero (frah-kee-tay-ro)
From the Spanish *fregado,* meaning "annoying", it refers to a person or animal that is pushy and reacts excitably; behaving in an over-friendly fashion.
He jes meet de girl an' he gettin' on so fraquitero!

frazzle
To upset someone; untidy-looking.
Jes so yuh come an' frazzle mih up!

freeco
Anything that is acquired freely.
We doh use 'freeco' no more as it gone out wit' de dinosaurs.

free paper burn (free pay-pah bun)
It means that holidays have ended and it's time to return to school.
Ah cyar believe de vacation done an' all meh free paper burn.

free sheet
The same as *carte blanche,* it means one is unfettered.
He come in de house an' take 'way everything free sheet.

free up
To let loose; to let down your hair or your guard.
Is time to free up yuh body an' take off dem tight clothes.

French Creole
Used to distinguish the Caribbean-born French planters from the British planters.
Everybody so mix up now it hard to tell who is French Creole!

frenin (freh-nin)
The friendly relationship between a man and a woman; usually consenting indivduals in a sexual relationship.
Since de day he land in dis country de two ah dem was frenin'.

fresh cold
A newly-acquired virus that leaves you sneezing and coughing. Trinis aptly name a new virus according to a popular event of the time.
Watch yuh doh give meh dat SOE fresh cold yuh hear!

freshness
It is often used to mean words or acts of sexual harassment. It is seldom used as "new and clean".
Yuh know mih boss go an' bring he freshness to me!

fresh water yankee
A Trinidadian who returns from the USA or elsewhere with an American accent after spending a short time abroad.
Yuh know Hafeeza gorn England but she come back talkin' fresh water yankee!

frig up
Full of oneself; pompous; to spoil or damage something.
Is you who gorn an' frig up de washin' machine?

frighten Friday
A state of timidity and nervousness.
Why yuh frighten Friday so chile. Come in here, nobody go eat yuh!

frizzle fowl
A common breed of yard fowl distinct because of its unusual ruffled feathers.
Yuh shame mih at de people weddin' when yuh come lookin' like a frizzle fowl.

frontin'
Someone who is pushy and who attracts attention to oneself.
Little boy, know yuh place an' stop bein' so frontin'.

froupsy (frup-see)
A carelessly clad person; dishevelled looking.
See how dah nice gyul change an' come so froupsy-lookin'!

fry dry
A small herring fish.
Gimme a half-pound of fry dry so ah could team it up wit' some tamadole choka for lunch.

fudge
A hard milky chocolate candy; to copy.
Doh go an' fudge de exam an' make de teacher fail yuh!

Fuh troot?
Is this true? Really?
Fuh troot? Yuh mean she up an' leave he high an' dry?

full ah mout'
"Full of mouth" means capable of bragging; plenty *ole talk*.
Dem only full ah mout' talkin' 'bout how dem win de match.

fus / ah fus ah
A creole term used for emphasis; to underscore a point.
Ah fus ah did love she! Ah coulda dead for Marian one time!

G

gallery
From the French *galerie* , "to pass the time of day", it also means to show off oneself and be seen.
She take up modelin' because from de time she born she did like to gallery.

gambage (gam-baj)
From the French *gambade,* "to skip about" or "to frolic", it now means cocky or to show off.
Dat family too full of gambage for mih.

gayap (gai-yap)
Of Hindi origin,the old village custom of teaming up to help build a house, or a community centre or protecting Nature.
Let's make sure we have food for when we hold de gayap dis weekend.

gayelle (gai-yel)
The patois word for "a pit" or "a yard", where cockfights are held; the name of a Trinidad television station.
In dem days we used to go wit' O'Halloran to de gayelle up in Valencia forest.

Gaza Strip
The night spot along Wrightson Road popular for its ladies of the night and other offerings during the war years.
Is de fightin' dat give dat place de name of de Gaza Strip.

gazette
The name of a now-defunct newspaper; a source of government information; old newspaper used for wrapping.
De Gazette publishes information from inside de government.

geera (jee-rah)
Tiny seeds of cumin popular in East Indian cooking.
Roast de geera in de fryin' pan before yuh put in some dhal.

Geezanages! (jeez-an-ages)
An exclamation of wonder or bewilderment, which means: "Oh my gosh!" or "What a shame!"
Geezanages! West Indies get lick down jes so!

Geeze-u-web! (jeez-u-web)
An exclamation of dismay or wonder.
Geeze-u-web! Yuh wearin' dat same ting to go an' meet de Prime Minister?

georgie bundle (jah-jee bundle)
Anyone who trundles little parcels around like an old person toting possessions; a little baby in arms. *Jahajee* in Hindi refers to the ship bringing early immigrants.
She leave de hospital wit' she little georgie bundle for de third time.

geritout (jer-ree-tout)
A shrub with leaves that are boiled to make tea, known as a cure-all for colds and eye infections among others illnesses.
Ah go make some geritout tea for yuh jes like Granny uses to do.

get away
To escape; to have a dispute with another.
Yuh mean to say yuh let de damn fish get away! Well now yuh an' me go really have to get away!

get fire
To lose your job.
Yuh go an' get fire because yuh always sick an' does reach to wuk late.

get on
To make trouble; to get into an argument; to misbehave.
De mister start to get on bad when he hear fares raise in de maxi taxi.

gibberish (gib-bridge)
Distortion of English words so as to spin a pidgin dialect that is really funny and meant for private dialogue
"I am going with you" translates into gibberish "ap-pai apam go-po-ip-ping wip-it you-pou".

gig
An entertainment event.
Kes an' de band had another gig in LA so we travel up wit' he.

gigiree (gee-jeh-ree)
A busy person; a nervous person; of diminutive size.
Get yuh gigiree little self outta here before ah give yuh some wuk to do.

gil gil
To mock someone; to laugh at someone else's misfortune.
Yuh goin' gil gil but de same ting coulda happen to yuh!

gimme a fat chance
Leave me alone; don't bother me.
Gimme a fat chance an' doh bother meh for no lotto money.

gimme gimme
The insatiable demand for money and hand-outs.
De trouble now is dat too many gimme gimme people does depend on de government freeness".

gingay (jin-gay)
To call a hex or bad luck on someone.
It have so much gingay on he head so dat is why he cyar see he way.

glassmaker
Used to ask the question whether one is transparent.
Yuh fadder is a glassmaker? Yuh in front de TV an' ah can't see nutten!

goat (ghost)
The way that "goat" is pronunced at an East Indian wedding. The curried "goat" usually turns out to be mango.
Hey Dool, put some ah dat curry goat on de plantain leaf.

goat mouth
Blight in forecasting something bad.
Ah feelin' better now so doh go an' put goat mout on mih so ah cyar come to de fete tonight.

goat racing
A popular sport in Tobago.
Ah bound to go goat racing in Tobago dis weekend.

goblet
A water cooler made of clay with a teacup spout.
Yuh know how long me eh see a genuine water goblet.

god horse
Also known as the *Praying Mantis*, an insect with stick-like form resembling a kneeling horse.
De god horse come an' rest on mih jacket like is a sign of somethin'.

God res' de dead
Passive and non-committal.
Chris eh take after he fadder at all. He's a real God res' de dead.

God sen'
An unexpected reward.
Dis Western Union from Tantie in Brooklyn is a real God sen'.

go forwards
To move ahead.
Go forwards an' make way fuh dem udders who marchin'.

goin' to do for you
I will get even.
So help meh God ah goin' to do for you so yuh doh get nutten Mammie lef we!

go 'long
If one continues in one's way, one will meet one's just desserts.
Go 'long behavin' like a Bad John an' you go make ah jail.

gone orf
Gone mad; or to get excited over something or someone.
If yuh see how Tricia gorn orf on she new boyfriend!

gone through (gorn troo)
Beaten up; or dead.
Yuh see dis handbag yuh give mih here, like it gone through oui.

good fuh nutten
Someone who is good for nothing.
Dah good fuh nutten husban' show up month end wit' he two hand empty.

good fuh yuhself
One can take care of or defend oneself.
Me eh able wit' you nuh, yuh too good fuh yuhself!

good too bad
To emphasise a point, it refers to one's degree of aptitude, often used in praise.
Hear nuh man! When it come to talkin' politics yuh good too bad!

go 'rong (*see* dress down)

go to town on it
To describe the details to which somebody's problems will be aired.
Now dat de results come yuh go hear dem go to town on it 'bout how de teacher couldna teach.

governor plum
A fruit with a hard seed, green when young, pulpy when ripe.
Yuh know dem CEPEP workers go an' cut down de governor plum tree by de ravine on de Diego Martin highway!

grab
A game of cards that tests the player's ability to win all or most of the pack.
De only card game ah know good is how to play grab.

gracious
A reluctant appraisal.
She bring she gracious daughter here to show she off.

grand charge
Talk designed to hide or to lead away from the real issue at hand; making much ado about little.
Is only grand charge he does make when time come for he to pay he share of de bill.

grease hand
To bribe.
Is true to get help in dem government office yuh must pass a grease hand?

greasy pole
An old-time village sport of oiling a pole or tree for competition to see who could shimmy up the fastest.
Yuh mean yuh doh remember greasy pole in de sport ground long time!

Green Corner
Popular meeting spot at the corner of Park and St. Vincent streets in Port of Spain.
The chant use to be "Mastifeh Mastifeh meet me down by de Croisee, Cutoutta Cutoutta meet me down by Green Corner".

gri-gri
A small greenish grey or yellow fruit of palm variety, the seeds of which yield a hard coconut type kernel.
When ah tell yuh ah did love to eat gri-gri in de country.

grind
To stifle one's feelings, thoughts or actions.
Ah had was to stay an' grind while Fatboy show off he new gyul.

grip
A suitcase; a piece of luggage.
If yuh know how ah vex ah did lose mih good grip when ah change plane in New York.

grog
A swig of rum or any other alcohol.
Hey Chin, gimme ah grog dey. Charlie go pay.

gros michel (gwa-mee-shel)
From the French meaning "Big Michael", a sweet and popular variety of banana.
Gimme dat hand of gros michel over dey.

ground itch
Any irritant that causes the victim to scratch the feet incessantly; a parasite that lives in dry earth.
Yuh gettin' orn like yuh have ground itch!

ground provision
Any of the root tubers like potatoes, yam, dasheen, tannia, cassava.
Prepare de ground provision to make de sancoche.

gru gru boeuf (gru-gru-bef)
A small palm fruit with a thin brittle skin and sticky sweet pulp.
Meh eh too like de gru gru boeuf but mih little brudder cyar get enough to pelt.

guabine (wa-been)
A river fish that breeds frequently; a vulgar woman.
If yuh see dem women getting' on like guabine for Carnival! Dem too shameful!

guava season
Hard times.
In dis guava season meh cyar even take in a flim show like before.

guilpin (gil-pin)
A cutlass or machete.
Is only guilpin dem people does use when dey playin' bad.

Gumbo Lai Lai
A carnival character of yesteryear who prattled verbal expressions that were abstruse and meant to impress.
Since yuh turn lawyer yuh soundin' jes like Gumbo Lai Lai.

gundy (gun-dee)
The larger of the two front claws of a crab.
Watch when yuh cleanin' dem crab else de gundy go pinch yuh!

guppy
A tropical fish, known internationally and named after Dr. Lechmere Guppy, a naturalist who lived in Trinidad at the turn of the 20th century.
Go an' see after de guppy an' dem before dey dead in de fish bowl.

gym boots (jim boots)
The predecessor to the present day sneakers.
All ah we used to go out to school dress up smart in new gym boots when de term start.

gyul / gyal
A Trinidadian way to call out to a female.
Hey gyul! Wait fuh yuh boy nah!

H

had was to
More effective than "I had to", "I used to".
Ah had was to go an' visit Mama everyday in de hospital.

hair
The quality or texure of one's hair may be referred to as hard, soft, curly, straight, or wavy. There are other categories like "dread", "rasta", "locks", "da da" or "peppergrains".
Look how mih chile hair change from soft an' curly to reel da da.

halay filay (ha-lay fee-lay)
From the French *haler filer,* "to push into a thread". It is a type of candy that stretches to great lengths.
De best longtime candy was halay filay.

half an' half
A state of being unwell; not feeling up to mark.
Today ah feelin' half an' half, is time for a good beach lime.

half-ripe
A state of immaturity in fruit or person.
Meh eh payin' one cent more for dis half-ripe zaboca.

half-white
A mulatto or light-skinned person with wavy or straight hair.
Blanca is de onliest one who come out half-white, de rest ah dem is dougla.

hamstring
Originates from the practice "to tie up and hang a leg of pork".
Mih mother go hamstring mih when she hear ah forget to buy de lotto tickets.

hand
A bunch of bananas; a weekly allotment of money for a *sou sou*.
If yuh see de nice hand ah plantain ah get yesterday!

hands down
The effort in getting something done.
Like everybody workin' hands down to fix dem flood roads.

happy like pappy
Blissfully happy.
She jes hear she pass de exam so she happy like pappy.

hard-back
Old.
Why she doh push dat hard-back mister to go find wuk.

harden
Difficult; stubborn.
Ah did warn she to stay 'way from bad company, but she too harden.

hardest
The superlative in goodness; to describe something appreciated.
Dat fete was de hardest.

hard head
Duncey.
Why yuh so hard head? Yuh cyar work out a little fraction sums!

harquai (har-kwai)
An ethnic mix between a Chinese and an Afircan, or other.
Dem little harquai bright too bad.

harass
To annoy or tease someone usually of the opposite sex.
Yuh get harass when yuh go on de beach in dem skimpy ting.

hasikara
Originates from Hindi, it is used in the form of "don't make hasikara",
which means "don't make too much fuss".
Doh make hasikara when he decide to fix up de apartment.

have it to do
To put up with.
Yuh have it to do in mindin' yuh sister chile!

head
To be clever.
Is head yuh givin' mih dere jes to borrow mih car?

head hot
To deal with many matters at the sme time.
*All yuh have mih head hot wit' all dem questions 'bout who right
an' who wrong.*

heckle
To tease or ridicule.
*Yuh like to give heckle but ah only hope yuh could take what
comin'!*

heise up
From the English *heist*, meaning "to steal". To lift up or remove
something or someone ; Trinidadians also say to "hef up".
Heise up de bag of cocoa so ah could weigh it on de scale.

high brown
Skin complexion.
Anton only have eyes for dem high brown gyuls.

high-class nonsense
Superlatively ridiculous commentary.
He fadder was de best Minister of Government dey ever had? Wha high-class nonsense he talkin'!

high daytime
In the middle of the day or in broad daylight; it can also mean "It's about time something was done".
Is high daytime dey should stop talkin' an' fix de roads in de country.

hip-tip
Someone with a lop-sided gait.
Since de accident if yuh see how she walkin' hip-tip!

hog plum
An acid type of plum good for making jams, jellies and wine.
Why yuh gorn an' cut down mih good hog plum tree?

Hollows
A favourite spot in the Queen's Park Savannah for lovers of Nature, romance or just meditation.
Leh we go an' take some pictures down in de Hollows!

hol' strain
To slow down; to restrain oneself.
Hol' strain Miss Lady, de officer comin' to take yuh complaint.

hoop
An old-time game of hide and seek played by children.
Leave de children alone. Yuh eh see dey playin' hoop in de yard?

hop
"To make one hop" is to keep one busy or to give one trouble.
Oh gorm, when yuh sick so yuh does make me hop.

hops bread
A small round yeast bread originally baked in clay oven on banana leaves. Its crispy crusts and soft bread centre called "pet" from *pith* is not the same anywhere else in the world.
In London ah does dream 'bout hops bread back home.

hops scotch
A game played in schoolyards that calls for the children to hop along squares drawn in the sand.
Now dem children have laptop dem forget how to play hops scotch.

horn
The act of cheating on one's partner.
Believe me, dem kinda horn eh have nutten to do wit' motorcar!

horongo
A character of vulgar appearance and behaviour.
Stop actin' like a horongo an' go back to church.

horrors
Trouble.
Dis car givin' mih all kinda horrors to start.

horse whip
A green garden snake that is harmless.
Me eh care yuh say it harmless, ah 'fraid dah horse whip snake.

Hosay (who-say)
A Muslim festival that originates from the circumstances leading to the martyrdom of Hassan and Hussain, grandsons of the Prophet Muhammad.
We goin' down St. James to see de tadjah an' dem in de Hosay.

hot an' sweaty
Abrupt and without a plan; a rushed performance.
Yuh now come hot an' sweaty an' want to take mih to de pub!

hot foot
A person who is always off somewhere and can't stay at home for long.
Call Corinne before yuh visit as she hot foot too bad.

hototo (hoe-toe-toe)
An abundance of things.
When ah tell yuh it had hototo pigeon peas in de market dis mornin'.

hot pepper
Known as *Scotch Bonnet* in Jamaica and Barbados; this special variety of hot pepper is medium size, with crinkled skin and ripens to a red, yellow or green colour.
Put de hot pepper whole in de callaloo an' doh let it burst!

hot potato
To describe a sudden action of letting go.
After he pick up wit' Dolcie, he drop Tenisha like a hot potato.

hot shirt
To describe a man's colouful shirt.
Dah hot shirt wit' de palm trees an' ting remind me of Uncle Sebro.

hot up
To describe a sexy young girl.
Watch an' see how she go get she hot up self in trouble!

hound down (hong dong)
From the English "to hunt down", but Trinidadians give it a more sinister twist to mean persistent harassment.
Mih brother hound mih down for de laptop he lend mih last month.

house an' land
An individual's personal possessions.
Uncle Charlo comin' dis weekend to eat mih out of house an' land.

hurry hurry
A nonsense chant followed by "come for curry".
Ah love to remember when Mammy used to shout to we: "Hurry hurry come fuh curry".

I

Icenin' (i-suh-nin)
A sugary cake icing.
Ah used to eat up all de icenin' when mih mother use to bake cake for people weddin'.

icy hot
A thermos flask that can retrain heat or cold.
Ah still have a picture of Pappy goin' to work wit' icy hot.

I eh know
I don't know; also used as "me eh know". It implies ignorance on the part of the speaker; a negative response.
I eh know wha really goin' on in de Parliament!

immortelle
A large forest tree famed for its pretty salmon-coloured flowers and its timber. It is used as a shade tree for cocoa and coffee.
When ah tell yuh it does break mih heart to see developers cut down dem immortelle trees.

in ah rage
To rave about something.
Is fete in ah rage when we win de Windies Cricket match.

in de bamboo
To expose someone to ridicule or question.
He gorn an' throw mih in de bamboo when he say ah witness de robbery.

Indian Arrival Day
The East Indian Community celebrates this each year in May in memory of those immigrants who sailed on the first boat from Calcutta to Trinidad.
If yuh see how Indian Arrival Day is big celebration in Trinidad now!

in more trouble dan Brown
To experience more trouble than usual.
He in more trouble dan Brown now dat he drop outta school.

in pain
In emotional or mental woes.
Now dat we have new laws an' ting dem squatters in plenty pain.

in ting
To be involved in some intrigue or in a love affair.
Yuh could get yuhself in ting eh gyul! Wha yuh goin' around wit' dis new married man for!

in truth (in troot)
To question one's veracity or to reinforce it.
Yuh mean to say all yuh really come back to live in Trinidad in truth?

in two twos
In the quickest possible time; in a jiffy.
Ah comin' back to check yuh out in two twos.

in yuh glee
To your great delight; excited and excitable.
Yuh in yuh glee now dat de lawyer done read yuh husban' will!

iron
The percussion instrument in the steelband made from the brake hub
of a car.
De onliest steel pan ah does beat is de iron on j'ouvert mornin'.

Is dat!
In agreement.
A: *Is dat self ah did tell she 'bout living overseas. It eh easy.*
B: *Is dat!*

is me an' you
Both persons must settle a score.
Is me an' you if yuh doh bring home mih daughter before midnight!

Is so?
It questions an opinion; an observation.
A: *De Mayor say he serious 'bout movin' dem vagrant off de street.*
B: *Is so?*

it eh easy
It is not easy; things are hard; troubled times.
Wit' all we oil money it still eh easy nuh to get ah wuk.

it take you
It becomes you; it goes well with your dress style.
Dat hair colour take you nice, nice.

is you to ketch
You'd better watch out for yourself.
Look Mister, ah leffin' you an goin' Stateside. Now is you to ketch!

J

jab jab
From the French *diable diable,* devil devil, it is the refrain of masqueraders on *j'ouvert* morning.
Come leh we play jab jab next j'ouvert nuh!

jab molassie
Originates from *diable molasi,* meaning "molasses devil", it comes from old-time masqueraders who bathed themselves with the black gooey liquid on the first day of Carnival.
De first time ah ever play mas was when ah play jab molassie in Tunapuna.

Jack Spaniard (jak span-ee-ah)
A Trindadian name for a wasp. It used to be a reference to a lady's waistline. Now it is more appropriate to describe one with a bad temper.
Jack Spaniard must bite she as she temper jes like dem insects.

jagabat
An old-time word for a whore.
When yuh go out wit' mih doh wine up an' get on like an old jagabat.

jalousie (jah-loo-see)
From the French *jalousie,* a kind of venetian blind, that was popular as wooden window louvres for ventilation.
Go an' peep through de jalousie to see if Winston reach back.

jamette (jah-met)
From patois that describes a woman who displays lewd and raucous behaviour.
Yuh could tell dese jamette women anywhere.

jamming
Associated with loud music and feting; work overload.
Meh eh able wit' dis month-end payroll jamming! Ah goin' home early.

jam session
A crowded fete or a continuous playing of loud music; a traffic jam.
It go be one jam session if de Mayor doh regulate all dem street vendors.

jampe tampé (jam-tampay)
From the French *jambe,* meaning "leg", it refers to sitting with one leg crossed high over the other.
She was sittin' jampe tampé an' proppin' sorrow after de bad news.

jeera (*see* **geera**)

jefe (hay-fay)
From the Spanish meaning "chief"; a person of high rank or perceived high position.
Yuh get a little security wuk in de bank an' yuh tink yuh is a big jefe.

jep
A tiny wasp with a terrible sting; describes a person's character.
When ah tell yuh dat little gyul is a little jep. She rude too bad!

jes now
Just now, or in a moment; an indeterminate period of time; a favourite way of postponing something to be done.
Wait nuh man, an' ah tell yuh ah comin' jes now!

jes so
Just like that; a statement or an exclamation.
Yuh mean to say yuh breakin' up wit' me jes so?

jharre (jar-ray)
A Hindi word that describes the prayers over someone who is sick.
The pundit was movin' he hand while doin' de jharre over Premchand head.

jigger (chig-gah)
An irritating parasite that enters one's foot and causes intense itching.
Keep quiet nah while ah take out de jigger in yuh foot.

jim boots (*see* **crepesole** *or* **gym boots**)

jingay (jeeng-gay)
To cast a hex or a spell; associated with the occult; obeah.
Is he mother-in-law who put jingay on he for leavin' she daughter.

jingles
Thin gold bracelets.
Ah 'fraid to wear mih jingles to town now. It have too much tief.

jink toe
A sore toe.
Yuh better watch out fuh dat jink toe before it get worse.

johnny bake
A large round dough baked on a flat iron. Best when made with coconut.
Long time in Toco we used to enjoy Mavis coconut johnny bake with fish broth.

joke fadder (joke fad-da)
An attempt to be funny; a joke that falls flat or the father of all bad jokes.
Dah is joke fadder! Buh how come is only you laughin'?

jokey
Jokey-fied. Very funny.
Yuh too jokey! Yuh want to marry meh in six weeks! Yuh crazy or what!

jook (*see* **chook**)

j'ouvert (jou- veh)
From the French *jour ouvert,* meaning "day break". The early morning of Carnival Monday.
To play j'ouvert mas yuh mus be prepared fuh plenty mud an' ting.

jub jub
A sugar-coated candy made of gelatin.
When ah was little mih favourite sweetie was jub jub.

jukking board
The old-time piece of corrugated flat wood used to scrub clothes.
De jukking board stay jes so an' break since Frankie promise mih ah washin' machine.

Julie mango
A grafted mango with sweet flesh.
Mammy did like Julie mango de bes'.

jumbie
From the English word "zombie", meaning ghost-like.
Chile, doh go an' play by yuhself or jumbie go take yuh.

jumbie bead
A red and black seed collected from a pod and used to make
ornaments. Popular in Trinidadian handicraft and made into
necklaces, wristlets and anklets, and it is said to ward off evil spirits.
Make one ah dem jumbie bead wristlet for de baby.

jumbie bird
An owl whose nightly hoots foretell of impending death or disaster.
Me eh like to hear dem jumbie bird at all. It does spook mih out.

jumbie umbrella/parasol
Any type of mushroom.
*Watch yuh doh slip an' fall on dat jumbie umbrella growin' on dem
dead tree bark.*

jump high jump low
It doesn't matter whether your mind is already made up, something is
bound to happen.
*Jump high or jump low ah goin' to tell dem to cut de damn cable
service.*

jump up
To dance and prance with abandon; a fete or dance at Carnival time.
*How yuh could miss dat jump up at UWI wit' de President an' dem
comin'!*

jump up an' kiss me
A soft-stemmed plant with delicate flowers. It is used for medicinal
purpose.
*A little jump up an' kiss me is jes what de chile need to cure she
from all dem worms.*

juta (joo-ta)
From the Hindi *joohtaa,* meaning unclean food or drink. It refers to
one's saliva that remains on food or drink, the person sharing it is then
said to know all one's secrets.
*Dey say if ah taste yuh juta ah go learn all yuh secrets. Dah is true
nah?*

K

kachorie
An East Indian fritter made of *dhal*; also *cachowrie* or *katchowree*.
Ah now grindin' de dhal for de kachorie dat yuh like.

kaiser ball
A hard round candy with coloured swirls popular with children in the forties, probably named after Kaiser Wilhelm, Emperor of Germany.
Is a long time now since ah hear 'bout kaiser ball an' halay filay.

Kaiser William
The German Emperor referred to in the calypso of 1914.
"Run yuh run Kaiser William run yuh run..." was de catchy line in de calypso.

kaiso (kai-ee-so)
From the word "calypso", a native rhythm out of which song and dance evolved since the turn of the 20th Century.
Trinidad is de land of de kaiso witout question.

kaisoca (kah-ee-soca)
A combination of calypso and soca rhythms originating in the eighties.
Witout doubt Michael Rudder and Calypso Rose is de monarchs of kaisoca.

ka ka dent (ka-ka-da)
The remains of anything; leftovers.
He only leave me a little ka ka dent to pay de rent each month end.

ka ka nez (ka-ka-nay)
Of patois origin. Mucus stuck in nose; snotty-nosed.
We does call he Mr. Ka Ka Nez because he always diggin' he nose.

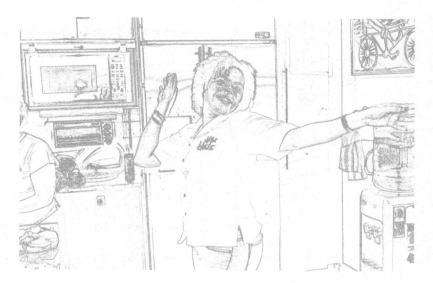

ka ka yank
Used to ridicule one who has spent a short time in the United States
but returns home with a false accent.
*Hear de ka ka yank nah! She say "Babbie went up de elly" for
"Bobby went up the alley".*

kalinda (*see* **calinda**)

ketcha glad
To suddenly become happy and excited.
Dis dog does ketcha glad anytime yuh come through de door.

ketch arse
to have a hard time making ends meet; to go through a rough time
financially. The same as "ketchin hell" or "ketchin mih nen nen".
He real ketch arse since he wife pack up an' lef he.

kick de bucket
The passing of someone.
Clifton stay jes' so an' kick de bucket when he reach home.

kicksin'
To fool around and have a good time. Its adjective is "kicksy".
Dem MPs eh tired kicksin' in Parliament?

kilkité (kil-kee-tay)
From the patois word meaning "tilted"; a state of being unstable; one
who acts stupid.
Since de accident he actin' little kilkité.

kill priest
Used in the negative to describe something too ridiculous to consider.
Walk 'round de Savannah in dat hot sun? Me eh kill no priest!

Kingdom come
To send someone to meet his/her maker.
*If yuh doh take 'way dis ole junk ah go sen' yuh to thy Kingdom
come.*

kiskidee/keskidee
A yellow-breasted bird so called from its whistle that sounds like the
French *qu'est-ce qui* (what is this), *qu'est ce qu'il dit* (what is he
saying).
*Is we who name we street Keskidee an' give all ah dem bird names
in Trinicity!*

Klim
A brand of powdered milk.
Is de old Klim tin dat he start usin' to beat pan.

knock about
To run around; to move from one place to another in idleness.
*Doh mind he dress up so. He used to knock about from pillar to post
before he win de lottery.*

knockin' dog
In abundance; a glut.
Up in Caura mango was knockin' dog last dry season.

kow tow
Originates from the Oriental custom of bowing to someone of higher
social status. To seek favours.
Is a mess to see how she does kow tow to all dem high-up people.

krick krack *(see* **crick crack**)

kuchoor (see **cuchur**)

kurma (koor-ma)
An East Indian or Middle Eastern delicacy that is a crisp candy made from flour, deep fried and coated with sugar.
It have a ting in Chinee Spring Festival dat taste jes like we kurma.

kurta (koor-tah)
A long pants typical of East Indian dress.
Vijash why yuh not wearin' yuh kurta pyjamas tonight?

kyar/cyar
Trinidadian dialect for "cannot" or "can't".
Me cyar bother mihself wit' dis distraction! Ah goin' Tobago to chill out.

L

la basse
From the French meaning "down below". It refers to a garbage dump, in particular the main waste disposal area south of the Beetham Highway and east of Port of Spain.
It beat me why anybody coulda put de la basse out dey! Dem tourists tinkin' is a fowl farm.

la diablesse (la jah-bles)
A devil woman or "she devil". A folk lore character, a beautiful woman who tempts men after their late nights out. She is recognized by her cloven hoof.
Pappy use to say is la diablesse who get he good an' proper when he wake up to find heself in a cemetery.

lagahoo
From the French *loup garou,* meaning "werewolf". A folk lore character who prowls around at nights.
She stop limin' late in Grande since she realise dem lagahoo is real bandit.

lag
"To take lag" is to upbraid another.
When ah give mih fadder de results he go take a lag in mih tail.

laglee
From the patois meaning "glue-like", the sticky sap from a *chataigne* or *breadfruit* tree.
Mih sister boyfriend stickin' on to she like laglee.

lagniappe (lan-yap)
From the Spanish *la napa,* meaning "something added".
Throw in two grain of peas extra for lagniappe!

lahay
To idle, to gawk, or to lime.
Me eh have no time to lahay wit' all yuh dis mornin'.

lakatan / lacatan
A variety of bananas.
Yuh eh see dis big bunch of lakatan ah buy in de market?

lambie
A type of conch for making souse, stews, soups or curries.
Ian go spend de whole day catchin' lambie in Tobago.

land up
To end up.
How dis box land up on mih desk? Me eh eat no fas' food today!

la pli qu'a vini (la-pli-ka-vini)
From the French *la pluie qu'a venir,* meaning "the rain is coming".
La pli qu'a vini or *la pli qu'a tombé is de same dam ting. It mean de rain comin' or it go fall jes now.*

lappe (lahp)
A small wild animal prized as a culinary delicacy.
So when all yuh hunt out de lappe, what go lef fuh nex year?

las' lap
The surge of energy expended in jumping up on Carnival Tuesday night.
Leh we ketch a las' lap with Phase Two in St. James nuh.

las' train
The Las' Train to San Fernando is a calypso by Lord Dictator in 1950.
Imagine singing de Las' Train to San Fernando wit' dem ole Trini friend we bounce up in Hong Kong!

lavway
From the French *la voix*, meaning "the voice"; early form of calypso, with singer and audience interacting.
Dem ole timers say lavway was de earliest version of Calypso.

lay lay stick
A swizzle stick that is used also as an instrument of correction in the old days; the predecessor to a blender when making callaloo.
Is de lay lay stick dat we use to get on we bottom dat have we straighten out today.

l'ecole biche (see **biche**)

leggo
Let go; to dance and have a good time.
Come leh we leggo an' forget de rest ah dem.

leh we go
Let us go.
Come leh we go down de road an' lime nah man!

level so (*see* **jes so**)

lick down / lick up
To knock down with fierce intent; to eat greedily.
Look how he lick down all mih leftovers! Now ah feel ah could lick he down!

lickrish
Greedy; an insatiable appetite.
He too lickrish. He eat up all de bake an' eh leave none for he sister.

licks / licks like fire
The fast pace of a game in favour of the winning side; a beating.
Look nah man! It was licks like fire by de West Indies in de Oval dis morning.

like ah tick
Attached, similar to a parasite on its host.
Watch it boy! Me eh like nobody to hold on to me like ah tick.

like ah ting
To like confusion and intrigue; to create *ole talk*. However, "to be in ting" is to be involved in confusing events or in a love affair.
Doris like ah ting too bad so dat is why she always have to be explainin' sheself.

like bush
An abundance of anything.
It have sale like bush goin' on now dat Christmas over.

like God res' de dead
A state of quiet similar to a dead person.
Vilma marry a man who lookin' jes like God res' de dead.

like salt / like saltfish
To be involved in many things; to appear everywhere; a popular person.
Now dat she in government she come jes like saltfish an' she on all de TV programme.

limbo
To dance under a cross bar without touching it. The best dancer must pass under the bar at its lowest with body bent backward. Trinidad lays claim to this performance.
Yuh eh know de limbo is a dance from Trinidad.

lime
To pass time in idle pleasure. English sailors were known as limeys who sucked limes to prevent scurvy. They used to line up while waiting their turn outside of brothels.
Come leh we make ah lime down by Smokey an' Bunty's in St James.

lime bud tea
The brew made from young leaves and flowers of the citrus tree.
Plenty ah we grow up on lime bud tea.

lingay (ling-gay)
Long and thin and wiry; a description of a lean person.
Move yuh lingay self from out of mih way.

lionel
A spin on the words "to lie" that describes a liar.
Yuh is a real lionel, comin' an' tellin' me yuh give me back mih money.

lipay (lee-pay)
A Hindi word, meaning "to plaster the wall with a mixture of dirt and cow dung".
Leh we lipay de walls now before it start to rain.

Little Englan'
In Colonial days this meant "to beat around the bush" or "to bramble", in which case the speaker was said to take you to Little England. Also a nick name for Barbados.
Yuh hear Little Englan' now reach develop country status? Doh play wit' dem bajan!

live in
Followed by "yuh tail" or "yuh skin", to describe a great deal of persistence.
Me and yuh fadder go live in yuh tail to get good marks in school.

locho
An abominably lazy person; a parasite.
Move yuh locho self from de couch leh me clean down de place.

loll off
To relax with limbs outstretched; to spread out.
Doh go an' loll off on mih good bed spread an' rumfle it up.

long eye / eyes too long
A man who has the roving eye.
Mih husban' have one fault, he too long eye.

long streak ah misery
A tall chap who gets himself into one calamity after another.
Lo and behold mih daughter bring home dis long streak ah misery an' say is she boyfriend.

long time
A long time ago; in the good old days.
Long time it didna use to have all dis setta criminal behaviour in we country.

Look nuh!
An expression to denote annoyance; or a statement to take note.
Beware or watch out!
Look nuh! It eh everytime ah go fork out money to pay for yuh gas.

Lord put ah hand! / Lord have mercy!
An exclamation that asks God to take pity; an intercession.
Lord put ah hand! Dey come an' drive de tractor over mih good sweet potato.

lorse away
To get lost; or to become dissolved and disappear.
All de crab get lorse away in dis big pot of callaloo.

lota
An East Indian vessel for flower offerings used at prayers and festivals.
Ah gorn an' lorse mih nice brass lota wha mih boughie did give mih.

lotah
White skin spots caused by a calcium deficiency, or by a fungal infection.
How come yuh gettin' dem lotah spots on yuh skin? Go an' see de doctor quick, quick.

love vine
A parasitic creeper whose yellow tendrils choke any bush it comes into contact with. An extreme case of love sickness.
How yuh clingin' to he like a love vine? Dem ting doh las'.

low
A stingy and miserly attitude; penny-pinching and petty.
I doh do business wit' any low person like yuh uncle. He go dead bad.

low class
Extremely bad manners; loud and vulgar behaviour; poor standard.
Me doh meddle wit' dem kinda low class people at all.

Lucifer
The devil character Beelzeebub played at Carnival time with huge head piece and costumery. He carries a book and a pitch fork in hand.
Lucifer an' he imps is de onlies' kinda mas we use to play long time.

M

mabouya (ma-boo-ya)
A house lizard also called wood slave or *twenty four hours*; a harmless insect-eater. Elsewhere it is called *gecko*.
Leave de mabouya alone. It only eatin' insects.

ma ca fourchette (ma-ka fou-shet)
From the French meaning "what's stuck between the fork"; leftovers.
No pot sweeter dan a good maca fourchette.

ma chère (ma shay)
From the French meaning "my dear"; a term of endearment; to show surprise.
Ma chère, if yuh see de high price of tings in town now!

macajuel (ma-ka-wel)
A large snake found in country areas, well known for long rest periods after satisfying an enormous appetite.
He stuff heself full of pelau, fry chicken an' booze so now he sleepin' like a macajuel.

macco / maco (mak-ko)
Nosey; or a nosey person; superlative description of size.
In every Trini is a macco waitin' to crawl out!

macomere (ma-ko-meh)
Of French origin; the godmother of one's child.
Ah goin' to visit mih macomere in La Brea. Is she who stay for mih chile!

macomere man (ma-ko-meh man)
A man who likes to meddle in women's affairs; an effeminate man.
De fight start when she call he a macomere man.

macometer (mako-mee-ta)
The degree to which someone else's business is monitored.
When de car did pull up wit' she an he, is now ah turn on mih macometer.

Mahal
A character of East Indian descent who found himself driving an invisible car around the country in the forties. It is said someone had worked obeah on him.
Ah have to practise for de drivin' test like Mahal and steer mih car all round de yard.

maigre (ma-gah)
From the French *maigre,* meaning "thin and scrawny".
How come yuk lookin' so maigre! Like yuh wife gorn on strike!

make ah jail
To spend time in prison.
Go on wit' yuh nonsense an' see if you doh make ah jail!

make back
To make up; to resolve a conflict.
De two ah dem love birds make back good, good now.

make ole style
To show off; to pretend that one is more important than others around him/her.
As soon as he step off de plane at Piarco one time he start to make ole style.

make out
An act of surviving.
Doh worry 'bout me, ah go make out as usual.

makin' hot / cold
The state of the weather as it affects one.
Open de window nuh, it makin' too hot in here.

mal ochay (mal oh-sher)
From the French *mal odeur,* "bad scent".
All yuh children go an' bathe, all yuh smellin' mal ochay.

maljo
From the French *mal yeux,* meaning "evil eyes". The blight that
befalls someone or something when given the "evil eye". Blue or
black jet beads on a baby's wrist will keep away the evil.
Mih orchid plant was growin' nice, nice until she give it maljo.

malkadee
From the French *mal qu'a dit,* meaning "sickness of sorts"; someone
or an animal who has caught a fit as in epilepsy.
De dog start to tremble like it was catchin' malkadee.

Mama de l'eau (ma-ma glo)
From the French, meaning "mother of the water"; it describes a
serpent sitting on a tree branch, combing long hair, while guarding the
river water.
*If yuh see how nice Alf Codallo did paint Mama de l'eau and dem
other folk lore characters!*

mama tater (ma-ma tay-tah)
A fresh water fish with a wide mouth.
She with she mama tater mout does talk too much.

mamaguy
To laugh at or to ridicule tongue-in-cheek.
Dis eh no mamaguy eh but yuh really lookin' sweet dis mornin'!

mamapoule (ma-ma pool)
From the French *mama poule,* meaning "mother hen". Used to
ridicule a man with effeminate tendencies; a fussy male or one
preoccupied with domestic details; a hen-pecked husband.
*Marva turn Marvin into one mamapoule man. We use to call he
Marva and she Marvin.*

Mamayo!
An exaggeration of bigness; an exclamation of surprise.
Mamayo! Look at dat big pumkin yuh have in yuh garden!

mamey apple
A large brown fruit with yellow pulp. Its seeds grounded and mixed
with rum were used to treat lice.
Grannie use to treat we head wit' mamey apple medicine.

mamey sapote (mam-ee see-pote)
A large brown fruit related to the *sapodilla*. The firm sweet flesh is used for making jams and preserves.
Down St. James dey does even sell mamey sapote icecream.

mango
A tropical fruit that comes in many varieties: julie, graham, rose, zabricot, dou douce, teen, vert, calabash and starch.
Anyone who could pelt mango like you should talk to Brian Lara.

mango chow
A snack of sliced half-ripe mango with salt and hot pepper.
Dis mango chow hot like fire!

manicou (ma-nee koo)
A forest rodent prized as a table delicacy during hunting season.
It eh have no way ah eatin' manicou outta de huntin' season.

manicou gros yeux (ma-nee-koo gwoze yeh)
From the patois meaning "manicou – the rodent with big eyes"; used to describe someone with bulging eyes.
De chile come out jes like he fadder wit' manicou gros yeux.

manos manos
From the Spanish meaning to match you "hand for hand". It means a confrontation with fists; straightforward; no nonsense.
Dah is how it movin' wit' me, we go settle dis manos manos.

mapepire (ma-pay-pee)
A poisonous snake. Along with *mapepire balsain* and *mapepire zanana*, they belong to the notorious pit viper family.
Doh trouble she nuh! She does bite like mapepire!

marabunta
A type of army ants that reacts viciously when disturbed.
Is dem marabunta self dat bite up she foot.

Maracas (ma-ra-kaas)
The beautiful beach of Maracas Bay on the north coast.
Yuh eh hear de Minister of Works want to dig a tunnel through de mountain to Maracas!

marasme / mirasmee (ma-raz-mee)
From the English word *marasmus*, to describe a state of poor health; thin-looking; impoverished.
Now we have all dem wellness clinic it eh have no more marasme-lookin' people in de country!

marchand (mar-shan)
From the French meaning "vendor".
De mayor try to move all dem marchand on Charlotte Street an' if yuh hear how dem people gettin' on!

maribone (ma-ree-bone)
A tiny wasp.
Ah doh know how ah tangle up wit' dat maribone nest, but Lawd ah get sting!

Marine Square
The original name for Independence Square was *Plaza de Marina*. It was laid out in 1816 by Sir Ralph Woodford at the southern end of Port of Spain.
Dem eh tired change de name of dat place! Marine Square change to Independence Square an' now it call Lara Promenade wit' he statue.

marish an' parish
All and sundry; everybody.
Now doh go an' tell de marish an' parish ah gettin' married to Robbie.

mark bus'
To burst the mark as in a game of chance; to let the cat out of the bag.
When de mark bus' yuh go see how many people tief.

mas (m-a-as)
From the French *masque,* meaning "to disguise"; to cover the face while indulging in the bacchanalian revelry of Carnival. Used to describe the state of wild abandon or madness.
On Carnival Tuesday when yuh see dem pretty costume, yuh bound to say "Mama dis is mas!"

mas camp
The place where a carnival band is planned and organized; the hub of
pre-carnival preparations.
Whey yuh say Tribe mas camp is again?

mash mout
One with a flat mouth.
Ah like yuh little sister wit' she cute mash mout too bad.

mash up
To break up something; to ridicule someone; to defeat.
Ah like how yuh mash him up in de debate.

Mash!
Go away! Get out of here! A command given to a dog.
Mash nuh dog! Get yuh stinkin' self out mih house ah jes clean up!

Massa day done
The days of master and servants are over. It makes reference to the
emancipation of slaves and was made famous by Dr. Eric Williams'
address in Woodford Square.
Boss! Massa day done so doh tell mih ah have to wuk overtime!

massala/masala
A combination of dried spices like tumneric coriander and cumin
ground together to form a paste. It is the base for curries from India
and South East Asia.
*Ah waitin all morning fuh you to bring de massala so we could start
we curry duck.*

Mastana Bahar
From the Hindi meaning "joyous spring"; the name of a popular
Trinidadian TV talent show.
Remember when Sham Mohammed was emcee for Mastana Bahar?

master do dat
One with particular tendencies, such as clumsiness or neatness.
Is Nigel who break up de wares. Yuh eh know he master do dat!

mataburo
From the Spanish *matar,* meaning "to kill", and *burro,* meaning "donkey". Thick red or green bananas, used in the 19th century to make banana flour. It is known as "man killer" as it is lethal when eaten while drinking rum.
Dem mataburo banana is reel dangerous so yuh better watch yuhself when yuh fire one!

matador
From the Spanish *matador,* "a bullfighter"; arrogant, determined.
He's a real matatdor when it come to sellin' he provisions.

matter fix
No need to worry; it's all taken care of.
De food done cook an' pack for de picnic so matter fix.

matuité (ma-twee-tay)
From the French *maturite,* meaning "mature" or "precocious"; over ripe or forced ripe.
She growin' big an' is so she matuité too bad.

mauby (mor-bee)
A drink made from the bark of the buckthorn tree.
Yuh eh know ole people say mauby good for diabetes?

mauvaise langue (mo-vay lang)
From the French meaning "bad mouth" or "bad talk"; speaking ill of someone.
She eh have no friends because she too mauvaise langue.

maxi taxi
A small passenger bus that transports people to different parts of the country as indicated by a particular colour band.
Ah notice de people who travel by maxi taxi well courteous. Dem does say mornin' an' evenin'.

Midnight Robber
A Carnival character, with a large fringed hat and a Robin Hood cape, who struts about with menacing whistle and words to terrorise onlookers.
Ah used to run an' hide when ah see dem Midnight Robber comin'.

mind yuh stops
To take heed; to watch oneself and one's behaviour; to correct one's attitude.
Mind yuh stops an' stop givin' me back answers.

ming piling (ming pih-ling)
A miserly, stingy, tight-fisted person.
Dat ming piling eh givin' one cent toward de birthday cake.

mingy (min-gee)
Stingy; cheap; parsimonious; a scrooge or skin flint.
Mih friend so mingy she does water down de orange juice for she guest.

minstrels
Carnival characters that mimic the Yankee troubadours in dress and song.
You does still see dem black and white face minstrels on de road on Carnival days oui!

miserable (mee-zeh-rab)
A state of being troublesome.
Dem children nowadays miserable too bad!

mister
A title given to an unaccustomed prominence.
What! Forty dollars for dat zaboca! He turn Mister Zaboca now?

mohong parao
A cocoa 'pagnol description of faeces.
Watch yuh step wit' dat mohong parao dem dog leave dere!

moi ca aller (mwa ka allay)
From the patois *moi qu'a aller,* meaning "I'm going".
Moi ca aller la calle moi translates into "Ah goin' home".

Moko
The wrath of a mythical being who is going to exact a price. Usually used with the phrase "the vengeance of".
Yuh see all dis crime an' ting and all dis flood we gettin'? Is really de vengeance of Moko for raping dem lands.

moko fig
Short, thick variety of bananas.
Is only when ah did go Arima by Tante Enecita, ah use to catch up wit' moko fig an' stew saltfish.

moko jumbie
An old-time Carnival character who dances on stilts, and is now popular in Carnival presentations and on the streets.
Doh tink is only in Africa it have moko jumbie! Ah see dem in China street festival too.

money jump up in ole mas
Money badly spent; the high cost incurred in playing mas.
We oil money does still jump up in ole mas no matter who in power.

monkey face
The act of pulling the lips apart and screwing up the face to imitate a monkey.
Yuh eh tired makin' monkey face behind de teacher back!

money satan
One who loves money and will serve the devil to acquire more of it.
She does eat an' dream of money, fus' she's a money satan.

monifato (mo-nee-fa-toe)
A spoilt child.
Me is one grandmother who eh mindin' no monifato.

monkey pants
To look foolish; or to get oneself into a tight spot.
He get heself into one monkey pants when he show up at de fete wit' dis new gyul.

monkey tricks
To try new schemes to overcome a situation; clever tactics.
Yuh eh hear de latest wit' dem con men, is like dem want to come back here wit' dey monkey tricks.

mook
A foolish person.
Come here yuh mook! Yuh eh know is only you ah love!

mooksie / mookish
Someone or something that looks beaten up; in the pits.
Me eh takin' dat mooksie umbrella to town wit' me.

mopper
One who sponges or takes advantage of another's generosity.
Yuh office friends is a setta mopper who does only come here to clean out mih fridge.

morish
The desire to have more of something.
When ah tell yuh, yuh home made bread tastin' morish.

morocoy
A land turtle that is kept either as a pet or prized as a table delicacy.
Take dat morocoy outside where he belong before ah trow he in de pot.

Morris chair
An old-time square-type wooden furniture.
Ah take off de ole varnish an' ah paint we Morris chair pink.

most present
To be obviously in the company of.
Yuh know de bold-faced tief was most present at de Company launchin'!

mountain chicken
An edible type of mountain frog popular as a delicacy in Dominica.
When ah tell yuh ah really enjoy dat mountain chicken by Parry an dem.

mountain dew
Illegally brewed alcohol.
Johnny, what kinda proof yuh make dis mountain dew with?

mouta
One who talks too much.
Doh listen to he. He's one big mouta always talkin' 'bout heself.

moxie
Dilapidated.
Dat moxie table is wha yuh call an antique! Yuh eh know dey make dat to look so!

much up
To make much of; to show unexpected affection.
Yuh comin' to much me up because yuh want money to buy a doubles!

Muslimeen
A Trinidad Islamic sect that stormed the Parliament on 27 July 1990 and held the country to ransom for six days.
Dat day when de Muslimeen an' dem try to take over de country it change we history for all time.

N

Nah!
No; an exclamation of disbelief.
Nah! Me cyar believe it have people who does win dat lottery!

nail jook (nail chook)
A skin puncture caused by a sharp metal object; usually a wound made by stepping on a nail.
Yuh know de Minister get ah nail jook when he visit de flood area.

namby pamby
A weakling; a derogatory term for one who gives in easily.
A: *Ah eh know how dah namby pamby get dah big contract!*
B: *How come yuh eh know? Is he wife family company.*

nara
A Hindi word for tightening in the lower abdominal muscles.
Like mih nara drop as it troublin' mih today.

nash
Thin and sickly looking.
When mih sister was little she was always nash nash.

navel string
The extent to which one is attached to his or her country.
She eh have to eat no cascadura to come back here as she navel string bury right here in T&T.

negue jardin (neg jah-deh)
The patois words to describe a yard or garden slave; portrayed in ragged attire during the carnivals of the nineteenth century.
Yuh come to de office lookin' like a negue jardin today.

nen nen
A term of endearment for godmother.
Go an' kiss yuh nen nen quick.

never see come see
One who acts or reacts excitedly over unexpected good fortune.
Yuh jes like a never-see-come-see wit' yuh new digital TV!

nimble
A parasite found under the tip of a fowl's tongue.
Yuh mean to say dese chicken get nimble again!

nine nights
Prayers on the ninth night after the death of a loved one.
Yuh buy crix, coffee an' sweet drink for Mammy nine nights?

no damn dog bark
A voice of authority that brooks no dissent.
Is Dr. Williams who say "let no damn dog bark" when he was talkin' to de people.

No nose Brackley
A person with a nasal or speaking disorder; a character with speaking impediment.
Alfie, yuh remind me of No nose Brackley when yuh tryin' to speak Yankee wit' yuh new false teet.

no probs
No problem.
No probs! Ah comin' to lime by yuh later.

North Stand; Grand Stand
Popular spectators' galleries for Carnival shows in the Queen's Park Savannah.
Is to see all colour pelau for Panorama Semis in de North Stand. Dey eh have any in de Grand Stand.

not me an' you
There is no likelihood that either of us will engage each other in chat.
Not me an' you to talk 'bout politics today.

now fuh now
Haphazard; not properly done; rushed and incomplete work.
If yuh see how de workmen does fix dem buildin' now fuh now!

nowherian (no-way-ree-un)
Of uncertain origin or pedigree; newly arrived.
Me eh know where Lucille pick up dat nowherian from.

Nylon Pool
A beautifully clear spot off Buccoo point in Tobago, ideal for snorkeling.
De Nylon Pool need plenty caring as is a fragile coral reef.

O

obeah (o-bee-ah)
Witchcraft; the occult; voodoo. The person performing the rituals is
known as an obeah man or woman.
Yuh should see who ah see hustlin' to go by de obeah man.

obzokee (ob-zok-ee)
Awkward; out of place; mis-shapen.
Dat new uniform have yuh lookin' obzokee.

Oh!
An exclamation; a genuine statement of surprise.
A: *Oh gorm! Look how he pants fallin' down an' all he jockey
expose!*
B: *No Ma! Dah is de new youth an' dem fashion!*

oh yo yoi
A cry of pain or delight depending on the circumstance.
Like ah hear dem singin' "oh yo yoi is Christmas again".

oil down
A dish made of breadfruit, pigtail and coconut milk.
Dou dou, whey yuh learn to cook oil down so?

ole duttiness
A good-for-nothing; a scamp.
Yuh let de ole duttiness come to visit he children?

ole mas
Old mask, or masquerade; the mas that is played on *j'ouvert* morning
when everyone dresses in old clothes and paint and mud; to overdo a
situation.
Dem politician make enough ole mas wit' we oil money.

ole talk
Chatter, not taken seriously.
Stop all dis ole talk now an' come leh we get dong to serious business.

ole tief
One with a reputation for dishonesty.
So why dey eh catch de ole tief an' throw he tail in jail!

one pot
Any combination of foods cooked together.
Is a little one pot ah makin' for lunch today.

one time
All at once; to get it over with.
Dis is one time me eh leavin' yuh to go no whey.

one to go
A call to a passenger to fill the taxi; the last drink before saying goodbye.
When yuh hear dem say "one to go" yuh better watch out for ah last round ah booze!

one day one day congotay (*see* **congotay**)

one today one tomorrow
The slow pace of accomplishing something; a lazy attitude.
Workin' fast? Uncle Verns does move one today one tomorrow when he cleanin' de yard.

one two three lavay
A chant accompanying a child's game of ball-bouncing.
Yuh have to say "one two three lavay" an' bounce de ball on de concrete.

only mout'
To show bravado with words and no action.
Is only mout' dem politician an dem have yes boy!

ordinary
Common or vulgar behaviour.
Keep 'way from dem ordinary people as dey only go lead yuh astray.

orhni (or-nee)
A thin long scarf draped around head or shoulder, tucked in at the waist and worn by East Indian women.
Matil always did wear she orhni even though she was dougla.

Oui! (wee)
From the French *oui,* it is an exclamation of assent. Trinidadians still end their statements with this reminder of the past.
Take care yuh fall down oui!

Oui fut! (wee foot)
An exclamation of delight or wonder.
Oui fut! How yuh dress up so today!

Oui papa/mama! Oui papayo/mamayo!
A combination of the French and Spanish to express surprise or delight.
Oui papayo! Dat is what Mammy used to say when she see Pappy deck off for church.

out off
To erase something or someone; to stop speaking to a friend; to leave.
Out off dem sums an' start all over again.

outside woman
A married man's mistress.
Doh mind he innocent looks, he done have ah outside woman.

overs
To end a relationship.
Is true ah did miss Imran, but ah now overs dat oui!

own way
To be stubborn; to refuse to take heed.
Patrick too own way an' ah tired tellin' he not to proceed wit' he vision.

oyster man
A roadside vendor who specialises in hot spicy oysters.
One time ah did hire de oyster man to bring he flambeau an' come by mih cocktail party.

P

pacro (pak-ro)
A mollusk popular in Tobago and supposed to have aphrodisiac properties; popular in soups as pacro water.
When yuh go Tobago be sure an' drink some pacro water.

pace like fire
Of great speed; often refers to action in cricket.
It was pace like fire wit' de West Indies an' dem visitors down in de Oval.

paime (pay-mee)
Of Amerindian origin. A cornmeal delicacy, sweet or salt, wrapped in banana leaves and steamed.
Ah cyar wait to head out by Tantie Louise for some good paime.

paipsey (paip-see)
Something that is not good or up to standard.
Ah fine ah lookin' so paipsey in dis outfit.

paleets
From the Spanish *palito,* "a short drink of alcohol"; used to show bonding with a drinking partner.
Give me a little paleets to steady mih nerves for dis piece of work.

palito
A drink of alcohol; introduced from "down de Main" and popular with cocoa 'pagnols.
Come leh we say Grace an' den down a little palito.

palm off
To pass the buck; to transfer responsibility.
Doh try to palm off yuh chile on me, Grandma goin' shoppin' today.

pan
The musical instrument made out of the steel drum. Originated in Trinidad around1940 and is tuned by heating and hammering sections to the required pitch.
At Keith funeral Boogzie make mih cry wit' he sweet pan.

pan side
A group of pan performers; pan beaters.
De whole ah Exodus pan side had to practise all night.

pannist
A solo pan performer.
Ah so glad mih godson Hayden an' all dem pannist gettin' a chance to travel round de world.

Panorama
The competition at Carnival time in which steelbands vie for the annual title of panorama champions.
How yuh expect mih to miss Panorama wit' all dat grog, pelau an' sweet music!

panyard
Home of the steel orchestra and the place where pannists practise.
Ah go ketch up wit' yuh by Despers panyard near the Savannah.

parlance / palance (pah-lance)
From the French *parler,* "to speak", which was made popular in the 2009 Carnival as a Road March by Soca Monarchs JW and Blaze who coined the term "palancing".
Wha is de name of dem singers who make palance de Soca hit?

Papa Bois (pa-pa bwa)
From the French meaning "Father of the Woods". This folklore character is depicted as an old man with a long beard who holds a young deer protectively.
Thank God Papa Bois does protect de forest an' wild animal from all dem slaughterin' hunters.

pappy show
To ridicule or to mock someone; an exhibitionist.
She does dress up like a pappy show to go to church every Sunday.

parade
To display oneself unashamedly; to strut about; to show off.
If yuh see how de boss parade heself in front de staff.

paradise plum
A candy that is round and of two colours.
A: *Yuh remember de sweetie called paradise plum?*
B: *Yeah man. Dey doh make dem so again.*

parandero (*see* **parang**)

parang
Originates with the Spanish influence when the *peons* worked on the
estates and plantations. They brought the Christmas tradition of
serenading as they went from house to house drinking and eating at
each stop-over. These serenaders are called *paranderos.*
*When dem parang did reach we all dem paranderos was stone
drunk.*

paratha
A plain *roti* or dough; extremely light and flaky and an
accompaniment to curries. Also known as *buss up shut* as it looks like
a torn-up shirt.
*Devi, yuh mean to say you eat out all de paratha an' eh leave none
for yuh fadder!*

park up
To lodge or to impose yourself on another; to stay in one place
seemingly to idle away the time.
*Curtis gorn an' park up heself like a statue down by Chow Chung
rum shop.*

parlour
A little shop that sells an assortment of anything but mainly cigarettes
and soft drinks.
De little girl went to de parlour for she mudder.

pastelle
A Christmas delicacy made of cornmeal in which there is seasoned
minced meat. It is wrapped in banana leaves and steamed.
Pastelle jes like de Venezuelan dish dem call ayaca.

pass in de rush
Lost along with everything else.
All meh jewellery pass in de rush wen dem tiefs enter meh house.

pass like bus
To leave someone waiting; to pass quickly without stopping or taking notice.
When yuh wit' yuh gyul friend yuh does pass mih like bus.

pass out
To faint or pretend to faint; also a cricket term.
Watch how dey go pass out when ah tell dem ah fire de wuk.

pass water
To urinate.
Grandpa fall from de ladder an' after dat he couldna pass water.

pass wind
The act of flatulence.
In de taxi de poor chile couldn't help but pass wind non stop.

patay poom
One who is fussy and complains over trivia.
She jes' like patay poom always stayin' home because she sick.

patchoi
A green leafy vegetable popular with rice.
Is plenty patchoi dat have dem Chinee people so slim!

patois (pah-twa)
A hybrid dialect from French, English and Spanish.
Yuh does hear plenty patois an'creole in St. Lucia an' Haiti.

pawpaw
Papaya, a tropical fruit.
Bring de pawpaw here an' leh we eat it.

peeny
Very small.
Why yuh givin' mih such a peeny piece of yuh black cake?

peewah
A small bright-coloured fruit from a palm. A snack when boiled in salted water.
Ah go have peewah for tea, breakfast an' dinner in de country.

pelau (pay-lau)
A popular Trinidadian dish. A pot of rice, pigeon peas, and meat, best when coconut milk and bits of salted meat are added.
It have pelau in all kinda colour in dem people picnic basket in de Savannah for Carnival.

pendejo *(see* **carajo)**
Dumb ass. It is a vulgar Spanish expression.
Mama was always callin' Uncle Sebas a real pendejo when he show up wit' de parang band for Christmas.

penny cool
A Trinidadian sweet drink in a plastic tube.
Since yuh behavin' so bad no more penny cool fuh yuh.

peong (pee-yong) / money peong
One who cannot control his or her urges; an addiction or obsession.
When ah tell yuh Daisy mother-in-law is one money peong.

pepper yuh skin / tail
To make your skin feel hot with blows as if rubbed with pepper.
If yuh doh listen to me ah go pepper yuh skin wit' licks.

petit bourgeois
From the French, also known as *petit bourge*, once used by the lower class to refer to the middle class who in turn aspires to the upper class.
Oui fut! Since yuh workin' in town yuh turn petit bourgeois!

petit carême
The short dry season in September, in the midst of the wet season.
It eh have no nicer time to visit Brasso Seco dan in petit carême.

petite bouche
From the French meaning "little mouth" or "mouthfuls"; to eat delicately with small mouthful or to eat small amounts of food.
Now doh play petit bouche for mih. Ah cook all dis food for all yuh.

Phagwa (pag-wah)
The Hindu celebration of Spring when revellers spray red colouring known as *abir* playfully on others. It is also known as *Holi*.
We goin' by Parbatee an' dem in Aranguez for Phagwa.

phantom
Any ghost or ghost-like character from the folk lore.
De man thin an' long an' lookin' like ah phantom from one of dem movie.

photo take-outer
A Trinidadian word to describe any photographer.
Come here an' pose quick nuh. Doh keep de photo take-outer waitin'.

physic nut
The fruit from a shrub known for its medicinal properties as well as its occult purposes.
Ah remember when Papa Laddie did use de ting call physic nut for he obeah.

pickney
A child; popular in southern United States with reference to a black or mixed child.
Ah doh know why dem woman makin' so much pickney dem cyar mind.

picky head / plaits
Matted hair.
Bring yuh picky head here leh mih comb it fuh yuh.

picong (pee-kong)
From the French *piquant,* meaning "to cut" or "to sting". For Trinidadians, this is the hallmark in hurling jokes at one another.
He could give good picong but he cyar take none.

picoplat (pee-ko-plat)
A small bird found throughout the islands, and is popular with bird lovers. Also known as the Grey Seed-eater.
Why all yuh take de poor picoplat prisoner for? Leggo de bird!

Pierrot Grenade
Of French patois origin, it refers to the old-time Carnival stick-fighter who parades on *j'ouvert* morning in rags and wire mas. A clown character who played with words and satire.
Is time yuh stop playin' Pierrot Grenade for j'ouvert.

pigeon peas
Known elsewhere as *congo peas*, or as *gungo* in Jamaica; they are green-shelled or dried. Popular in pelau and in curries.
Vic boy, yuh wife cook dis pigeon peas wit' real sweet hand.

pika
From the French *piquer,* meaning "to pierce" or "to prick". A thorn or sliver that enters the skin accidentally.
De chile start to bawl when de pika jook she foot.

pillow tree
A pillar or support beneath a building.
Aaron go an' help Daddy brace de pillow tree under de house.

pissin' tail
One who is having a hard time making ends meet.
De pissin' tail man have de gall to come an' aks me for a loan.

Pitch Lake
A natural wonder of the world in La Brea in south Trinidad. In Spanish *la brea* means "the tar". It yields alphalt and replenishes itself overnight.
Ah really wish dis government could fix up de Pitch Lake nice for visitors.

pitch
The black tar or asphalt that comes out of the earth and is used to pave roads throughout the world.
Yuh wouldna believe ah see Trinidad Lake Asphalt on barrels of pitch in de road works in China.

pitch oil
Kerosene; fuel for cooking and lighting lamps.
Doh make style now wit' yuh electricity, is pitch oil lamp yuh did grow up wit'.

planasse
From the French *planer,* meaing "to make smooth"; to hit someone with the flat side of a cutlass.
Did yuh see de news, farmers in Lopinot yesterday planasse reporters.

planten
A medicinal leaf used when dried for poultices, eye problems and sores.
Ah want some planten leaf to try out de medicine for meh eye.

platoner (pla-toh-neh)
From the French *planter,* "to plant"; to park up oneself somewhere that is unwelcome; to remain in one place for a long time.
Gyul, yuh really tink ah come here to platoner mehself in yuh house?

Play wid me/you.
A statement that elevates the speaker or the addressee to a new height of admiration.
So yuh get multiple entry visa to de USA. Play wid you!

play mas / make mas
To take part in the costumed revelry of Trinidad Carnival; to exhibit oneself in gaudy attire; to fool around; to take advantage of.
After Sahadeo dead de children make ole mas wit' he money.

playin' man
A precocious youngster.
Stop playin' man fuh me or ah go tell yuh fadder to fix yuh up.

please God
An entreaty.
We comin' to see all yuh Sunday please God.

poe / posie / pozie / posey / 'tensil
A toilet utensil still used for toilet-training children.
Grannnie posie used to be pretty for so wit' flowers an' ting paint up on de outside by de handle.

popo
A term of endearment for a baby.
Leh mih see if yuh popo come out like de fadder.

pock hand / fini hand
To ridicule one with a deformed or injured hand.
Doh go an' put yuh pock hand in mih lunch kit.

poke ah poke
Go slowly; don't overdo it; all's fine.
I dey ... ah goin' poke ah poke.

pois doux (pwa doo)
From the French meaning "sweet peas"; a large pod legume with
seeds in soft sweet pulp.
Ah bring down a nice pois doux seedling for mih town friends.

pol pique (pol peek)
From the French *pique,* meaning "sour"; a strong body odour.
Yuh smellin' of pol pique, boy when last yuh take a shower?

pommecythere (pom-si-tay)
A yellow fruit with spiked seed, good for making jams, jellies, and
juice. Golden *apple* in some other Caribbean countries. *Pomme* in
French means "apple".
Oh gorm! Dis pommecythere sour too bad!

pomerac (pom-a-rak)
A red pear-shaped fruit with a white interior. It is known as *otaheite
apple* in Jamaica.
If yuh see how expensive dey sellin' pomerac on de roadside.

ponche de crème / poncha crema
From the French, it means punch made of milk, eggs, rum and spices.
At Christmas time it contributes to the feeling of heady joy.
Phyllis poncha crema knock mih out good las' year Christmas.

pone
A sweet pudding made of cassava, sweet potato and coconut grated
together, sugared and spiced before baking.
Is all dat pone all yuh eatin' makin' all yuh so fat!

pong
To pound; to hit out or lash with verbal abuse; to bad talk or to
mauvaise langue someone.
Why yuh like to pong she so? Wha she do yuh?

pong plantain
Half-ripe plantain or bananas pounded into a tasty pudding for a side
dish.
*Is pong plantain an' callaloo ah goin' up Las Lomas to eat by mih
macomere.*

poom
Flatulence of any quality of noise or scent; also refers to the sound
from the steelpan.
Just listen to de sweet poom poom of dem tenor pans nuh!

poor great
A proud attitude adopted by someone of humble origin.
Dat family is one setta poor great from de time dey small.

poor guts
The condition in which the intestine is surprised by the improved
quality of food.
*Yuh went an' eat one setta rich food at de office party an' now yuh
poor guts actin' up.*

poor me one
Poor little one; the state of feeling sorry for oneself.
Tantie sittin' dey like ah poor me one so ah goin' to cheer she up.

poor white
Light skinned people who are down and out of luck.
Dem is poor white, but look at how dem big shot now!

Poposit (po-po-seet)
The patois name of an old-time flautist from Santa Cruz,
When ah hear Sonny playin' de flute it does remind me of Poposit.

Portugee (po-tee-ghee)
Someone of Portuguese descent.
Long time is mainly Portugee who did own rumshop.

pot hound (pot hong)
A mongrel dog; an insult.
De pot hound ah talkin' bout is not Rover, is yuh husban'.

pot spoon
A huge metal spoon used for stirring food in a pot.
Bring de pot spoon quick or we go have bun bun for dinner.

pow
Dumpling stuffed with pork, a favourite especially with Carnival revelers on *j'ouvert* morning.
We go stop for pow an' coffee before we hit Green Corner.

pound an' a crown
A ridiculous price charged for an item.
Everyting now cost a pound an' a crown in dem malls.

prophetess
A woman who gives spiritual succour to devotees.
De prophetess was gettin' a big church build for she in de heights of Guanapo.

proppin' sorrow
The forlorn position from placing one's face in cupped hands as if the whole world rests on one's shoulders.
Stop proppin' sorrow nuh gyul. De man comin' back nex' year for Carnival.

prostrate / prostate (pros-tait)
The male glands in the loin region.
Is dead he dead wit' prostrate cancer. De boy gorn jes so!

pulourie / phulouri / pulowri
An East Indian fritter, made of split peas. It goes with mango chutney.
Miss Dolly use to sell good pulourie an' is dat wha she use to send she children to university.

promasa
Ground corn flour used to make pastelles.
Long time we used to call promasa de corn flour mas for makin' pastelles.

pronto pronto / punto punto
From the Spanish meaning "quick quick".
Come back here pronto pronto after yuh deliver dem goods in town.

pulling bull
Private cars that work for hire.
Yuh eh know yuh coulda get fine for pulling bull?

push ah move
To become romantically involved.
Yuh know how long he did want to push ah move by me!

push come to shove
If there is no alternative, you have no choice but to yield.
Ah tellin' yuh if push come to shove ah go have to take de las' maxi taxi home.

push up
To describe someone who is embarrassingly a show-off.
See how he come an' he push up heself to take photo by de Minister.

put away de house
To clean and decorate one's living quarters.
Mih daughter cyar wait for Christmas to put away de house.

put foot
To step into a place.
Yuh eh go put foot inside mih yard until yuh say yuh sorry.

pwatik (pwa-teek)
From the French *pratique*, meaning "customer". Used to hail or to
address a customer or vendor.
Ay Pwatik, throw in some extra grain for lagniappe nuh!

Q

quackoo (kwa-koo)
All and sundry; the general public.
Every quackoo go know now ah takin' a boat cruise wit' she for mih holidays.

quale up (kwale up)
Shrivelled; old and tired.
Yuh expect mih to cook dem quale up dasheen bush for mih callaloo!

qualebay
Withered; thin; gaunt.
He come wit' he qualebay self to ask for mih daughter hand.

quarrelsome Mattie / meddlesome Mattie
A person who is fussy and complains a lot while interfering in another's business.
Know something? Dah woman is one quarrelsome Mattie.

quelbe (kwel-bay)
An old Congolese dance in Tobago in the thirties according to historian J.D. Elder.
Beryl McBurnie said that the quelbe was danced in Carriacou before it even come to Trindad.

quenk (kwenk)
A wild pig; a coarse and vulgar person.
Is dah quenk self who propose to me one time.

Qui dat? (kee dat?)
A mixture of French and English; who is that?
Qui dat? Is you Biptee who come to wake mih up so early?

R

Rabs Immortelle
A once popular Belmont band that attracted thousands of Carnival revellers.
Rabs Immortelle does do good work as dey does support plenty charity.

rachette / ratchette (rah-chet)
A cactus used for medicinal purposes.
Watch out for dem rachette dat have plenty picka.

raga raga music
The deafening music played by car owners.
Is time to fine dem car drivers who play raga raga music dat is a public nuisance.

rag up
To make someone look silly; to talk to someone in a harsh and demeaning manner.
She done apologise already so doh rag she up nuh!

rage
Ostentatious; overdone.
If yuh see how dem dress up in a rage to go to de concert.

rain set up
Dark clouds overhead.
Rain set up so yuh better take yuh umbrella.

rake
A juicy piece of gossip.
Hear dis rake nuh gyul. Tantie leave she husband.

rake an scrape
To eke out a living.
Man, you eh know what it like to rake an scrape all day long nuh!

ram cram
Crowded.
If you see how dem maxi taxi used to ram cram dey vehicle wit' school children.

Ramadan
The Muslim period of fasting that ends with the sighting of the moon and the celebration of *Eid ul fitr*.
De whole Mohammed family does celebrate de Ramadan.

ramajay
From the French *ramager*, "to warble" or "to chirp". To beat or flap the wings like a humming bird; to party.
Trinis can't wait to ramajay at a beach lime.

ramsack
From the English *ransack*, to search violently.
When we go see de end to dese bandit an' dem who does ramsack everyting when dey break an enter!

rango
Wild behavior, possibly from *orangutan* or ape-like behavior.
Yuh used to be so quiet, now yuh actin' like a rango.

ras naziboo
In the old days referred to a person with dread locks.
Go an' comb yuh hair as it have yuh lookin' like ras naziboo.

rasta / rastafari
A person who has adopted the lifestyle of the Rastafarian cult.
He gorn rasta now since he say Jah tell he dat all fruit belong to he.

ratiray (rah-tee-ray)
An old-time chant made popular by Designer's '92 calypso.
When de deejay start to play "Ratiray" is to see mas in de place.

reach me
To accompany me; to hand me.
Reach me to de corner, but like yuh want me to beg you or what?

red ants
Little red insects with a powerful sting. Used to describe someone
with a bad temper; skin colour.
Dah family is one set ah red ants. Doh tangle wit' dem at all!

red mango
A half-ripe mango pickled in a red brine.
*Doh forget to pick up mih red mango an' send wit Dexter when he
comin' Stateside.*

Red Solo
A Trinidad aerated beverage.
Pass mih a Red Solo to go wit' mih roti an curry mango.

reds
A light-skinned person; one of mixed blood.
Hey Reds, leh we take a drive up Maracas nah!

rent ah tile
The limited space occupied by two dancers in tight embrace.
Oui fut! De two ah all yuh dancin' rent ah tile. So wha goin' on?

Republic Day
A public holiday (24 September) celebrating Trinidad and Tobago's
attainment of Republican status.
Ah takin' it easy fuh so dis Republic Day.

repugnante (ray-poog-nan-tay)
From the Spanish word, meaning "repulsive"; to describe one with a
sour attitude.
*Dat security officer lookin' too repugnante for me to go an' ask she
direction.*

reverse back
To go backward.
Like yuh jes' buy yuh licence, yuh cyar even reverse back good.

rinse out
To wash and then put to dry.
Leh mih rinse out yuh clothes so it go smell nice.

Road March
The most popular calypso or tune played during the two days of
Carnival.
*Ah does still be hearin' de Road March poundin' in mih ears on
Ash Wednesday.*

roast bake
Tasty dough roasted over a fire or on a flat iron.
When yuh go finish de roast bake, Ma? Mih belly growlin'.

robber talk
Orginates with the Midnight Robber; to talk so as to show off, to
impress or to deceive.
Doh give meh all dis robber talk, Faizul, yuh cyar fool meh again.

romy (ro-mee)
A card game in which you knock table to indicate points.
Come leh we play some romy to pass de time.

roo-koo-tun-toonks
A fun word to describe backside.
*If yuh doh behave ah go hit yuh one lash in yuh roo-koo-tun-
toonks.*

roti (ro-tee)
An East Indian pancake recreated in Trinidad, a thinly cooked dough folded and eaten with curries; a national delicacy.
Come leh we go down by Girlie, she mother cookin' roti for we.

roucou (roo-koo)
A Trinidadian tree with spiky fruit and pulpy red seeds that produce a dye. It was the original "war paint" of the Caribs and it was used for food colouring.
Mentor an' Celestina did use plenty roucou in dey cookin' in Paria.

round de corner
An indeterminate point at right or left angle from where you are.
Mary say Mikey jes went round de corner to buy some fig.

rounds up
To gather; to bring together.
Is time West Indies rounds up a cricket team to beat de daylights out of Bangladesh.

rum cork
A boozer; a lover of the rum bottle.
Yuh sure to find de ole rum cork in Eli rumshop round de corner.

rummy
Someone who hits the bottle often; a drunkard or an alcoholic.
When ah used to see dem rummy comin' for Christmas so, ah used to hide even de bay rum.

rum shop
A popular village liming spot; a watering hole; a pub.
Ramsingh did live by Chin Fatt rumshop 'til straight so he drop dead one evening.

S

sa sa yae
From the French *ça c'est,* meaning "that's it"; an exclamation.
Ah remember Sparrow singin' in patois wit' he naughty sa sa yae kaiso.

sada roti
A thin bake or thick roti, accompanies a *choka* or a curry.
Me doh play no big shot nah, ah grow up on sada roti an' tamadole choka.

safe
A cupboard with wire mesh used for keeping food safe from predators.
Mih friend say de old safe does remind she of when she was growin' up in Tableland.

saga boy
A dandy. Peter Minshall strutted him off as a world character in the 1990 Carnival production of Saga Boy with girlfriend Tan Tan.
Yuh dress up like a real saga boy wit' fancy tie an' ting.

saheena (sa-hee-na)
An East Indian delicacy, made of split peas rolled in dasheen bush mixed in a batter and deep fried.
Try dis saheena wit' mango chutney, is ah real great appetiser.

sailor dance
A unique dance step that originated with old time masquerader dressed up in elaborate sailor costumes, imitated the crew stoking the ship's engine with imaginative dance steps using long iron rods.
Yuh cyar imagine how cute dem dancers look on stage doin' de sailor dance.

salamera (sa-la-mey-ra)
From the Spanish *sala mira,* meaning "dirty looks"; pushy.
He little daughter too spoil and salamera, me eh like she at all.

salop (sa-lop)
From the French *saler,* meaning "to trick a customer"; a lovable rascal.
Come an meet this salop uncle of mine.

salt fish / cod fish
An imported staple; one who turns up unexpectedly.
She come like saltfish an' most present in everybody lime.

salt kind
Salted meat in making *cook-ups*, soups and other Trinidadian dishes. Also called salt beef and pig tail.
Ah well remember dem barrels of brine wit' plenty salt kine in Chow Chung shop.

salt prune
Salty and sour preserved prunes imported from China.
Bet yuh eh know in China dem does put salt prune in a glass of wine to enhance de flavour of de drink.

same / sim
A flat green bean, popular as a side dish or in curry.
Is a little sim ah pick to go wit' mih sada roti for lunch.

same khaki pants / same ole' same ole'
Similarity or repetition of a situation; nothing new; it's the same thing all over again.
Sometimes ah does tink dat de new government is de same khaki pants when ah hear dem in parliament.

sancoche (sang-koche)
Known as *sancocho* from "down de Main", a thick soup made of ground provisions or root tubers, meat bones and dried peas.
Every Saturday was sancoche fuh de whole family.

Sando
San Fernando.
Yuh goin' dong Sando dou dou darling?

Sans Souci (sah-soo-see)
From the French meaning "without care", describes one of the prettiest scenic spots on Trinidad's north-east coast.
Ah want to spend Easter in Sans Souci dis year.

sans gout (sah-goo)
From the French meaning "without taste".
Dis stew tastin' sans gout; like yuh forget to put in salt or what?

santimanitay (san-tee-man-ee-tay)
From the French *sans humanité,* meaning "without mercy".
De chant of dat ole time calypso always did end with santimanitay.

santiwah (san-tee-wah)
From the Spanish *santa agua,* "holy water"; it is a ritual of sprinkling holy water over someone or some place to ward off evil or bad luck.
Like de Holy Spirit help she santiwah de place after de flood.

sapat (saa-pat)
From the Hindi *saapaat,* a slipper with heavy wooden sole and footband fashioned out of rubber from car tyres. Also close to the Spanish *zapata* meaning "shoe".
He put on he sapat to go down de road an' straight so he get knock down.

sapodilla (sa-po-dil-la)
A sweet fleshy brown fruit with rough skin and smooth shiny black seeds.
Is long time ah eh eat sapodilla so nice.

saroobhai
A Hindi word meaning brother-in-law – in particular the husband of your wife's sister/
He wife does favour the saroobai from St. Clair more than she own husband.

Savannah
Open grassland; Queens Park Savannah called the lungs of Port of Spain, it is about 232 acres and has a circumference of 2.5 miles.
We goin' up by de Savannah to kick some football.

sawine
An Indian delicacy of vermicelli, milk, raisins and spices, popular at Muslim festivals.
Saleema, de guests an' dem really enjoy de sawine yuh make for Eid.

say prunes
Used to describe someone who does not speak much but who turns out to be quite the opposite.
Mih mother lookin' like she cyar say prunes but doh step on she foot.

Scarlet Ibis
A national bird of Trinidad and Tobago; brilliant red in colour, it roosts in mangrove and feeds on shrimp.
Visitors bound to go an' see we Scarlet Ibis in de Caroni Swamp.

scotch bonnet (*see* **hot pepper**)

scruntin'
Hard up; down and out.
Dese days ah have no job an' ah scruntin' for so.

sea moss
A drink made from a type of sea weed.
Drink de sea moss nuh man. It go give you plenty iron.

seasonin'
A mixture of onions, chive, thymes, garlic and hot pepper that is used in West Indian cooking.
Is to leave de meat wit' all de seasonin' ah mince up, an' doh forget to put in salt.

seer
A clairvoyant; one who is involved with the occult or obeah.
Jestina gorn to de seer 'oman to see if she could find a husban'.

seewalaa
A Hindu temple; a place of learning.
Ah did grow up in Tunapuna close to de Seewalaa on de main road.

self / self-same
The same one or thing; used for emphasis.
Is he self who give me de self-same direction to come to see yuh.

semp
A popular cage bird, known as the *Violaceous euphonia*. The male is a good songster.
Like yuh happy today; yuh singin' like ah semp.

shabine (sha-been)
A light-skinned African with reddish hair.
Ah talkin' bout Riza de shabine gyul who mother had she wit' de white man.

shaddock
A member of the citrus family, similar to grapefruit, with reddish pulp. Its thick skin is preserved as a delicious candy in Trinidad.
Ah have a good recipe for makin' shaddock candy.

shado beni /chadon beni (sha-doe beh-nee)
A herb, also known as *colantro* or *cilantro,* that grows wild; used as a distinctive seasoning in cooking.
Add some more shado beni to de oyster sauce to make it nicer.

shakal / lookin' shakal
An untidy state; uncaring about one's appearance.
Ah find de men an' dem lookin' too shakal while de women an' dem looking nice too bad.

shalopeh
A cheap cloth, used for clothing slaves in the old days; used for sacking flour and sugar.
Is shalopeh trousers yuh great grandmother used to make for she children.

shandileer (shan-dee-lay)
From the French *chandelier,* meaning "candle stick", used to describe an ornate light fixture; a shrub for medicinal purposes.
Ah grow up in a house wit' a big shandileer but ah also know de shandileer bush yuh talkin' bout.

Shango
An African deity; a divinity of thunder, fire and lightening.
Leh mih tell yuh, Shango is one of de powerful deities of de Yoruba pantheon according to Molly Ahye!

shave ice
The snowy result from shaving the top off a block of ice; a feeling of self-pity.
Ah feelin' like a cent shave ice because ah use all mih money fuh lotto.

shining bush
A common garden herb used for making teas for colds.
Yuh gorn an' mash down mih shining bush tree dat ah does use for mih herb tea.

shrimps (strimps)
A popular crayfish.
Gimme a curried strimps roti fuh meh lunch today.

shoo shoo
Secret talk; to whisper in a conspiratorial manner.
All dem employees good to do is shoo shoo all day.

side board
Heavy piece of wooden furniture; a buffet cupboard in the dining area.
Geezanages! If yuh see cockroach in de old side board!

silk fig
A short silky smooth-tasting variety of banana.
Weigh out a pound of silk fig for mih.

simidimee (see-mee-dee-mee)
From the Latin *semi demi*, meaning "half and half"; fuss and bother; full of sound and fury.
Dis place have too much simidimee fuh me.

sit back down
A command.
Little gyul yuh in church. Sit back down an' keep yuh tail quiet.

size alls
An unbelievably large size in clothing.
De way she eatin' fas' food is like ah go have to buy she ah size alls in pants.

skilimineri (skil-lih-mih-neh-ree)
Persistent thinness; measly-looking.
Bonzo was one skilimineri piece ah dog from de Vet clinic.

skin
One's complexion, may be classified such as light or dark, brown or high-brown, red, black or white.
All she children skin come out different, some white, some black an' some brown skin in between.

skin teeth
To expose your teeth in a forced smile; a hypocritical smile.
Mammy use to say not every skin teeth is a laugh an' dat means all smile eh genuine.

skull(s)
Smartness.
Yuh usin' skulls again on yuh mother so yuh could go out an' play?

slave band
A gold bracelet that is broad and showy.
Yuh eh dare wear no slave band as dem bandit go relieve yuh of it.

small island
Any of the eastern Caribbean islands.
Plenty ah we have small island roots but we always puttin' dong each other.

smart man
A con man.
Ozzie is one smart man, he could charm de hair off yuh baldhead.

snat / snot
Mucus from the nose.
Bet yuh doh remember a sticky fruit call ol' lady snat?

snow ball / sno' cone / press
Shaved ice doused with colourful syrup, popular with itinerant vendors. Condensed milk added is also an option.
Is only now dem does call ah press ah sno' cone.

soca
A modern rhythm that is *soul* and *calypso* combined.
Come Mr. Deejay, give we some more soca tempo.

soft candle
Softened wax sold medicinally to make poultices.
A little soft candle will bring de boil to a head.

soft man
Easy-tempered; wishy-washy.
She an' she soft man goin' an' stay by she parents.

soi disant (sway dee-zah)
From the French meaning "so they say"; half-hearted.
He kept givin' me a soi disant excuse fuh not comin' to de party.

sometime-ish
Moody.
Ah doh bother wit' Brian at all. He too sometime-ish.

soot
Low hissing sound of air passing through the teeth; popular pastime of
limers who call out to someone in the street, especially a female.
*Long time men use to soot nice woman; now dey does tief dem
bracelet.*

Soparee Mai
A hybrid of the Roman Catholic festival with African, Hindu and
Spanish overtones; celebrated on the second Sunday after Easter. A
Madonna called "Siparia Mother" is the patron saint of Siparia.
De bus excursion leavin' jes now to visit Soparee Mai.

sorfee sorfee catch monkey
An easy way to win out.
*Ah tired tellin' yuh dat de way to get he to agree is to go sorfee
sorfee catch monkey.*

sore foot
To have an infection on any part of the leg; skin inflammed with
eczemas.
Mih father brother dead wit' one big sore foot.

sorrel
The red or white calyx of a plant that blossoms around Christmas
time; a drink made by boiling with spices and sweentened.
*Mammy does make a drink wit' de red sorrel an' wine wit' de white
one.*

sou sou
From the French, meaning "copper coin". A unique form of savings in
which members hand over a sum of money to one person over a
period of time, the total amount is then released to each member of
the group when his/her turn comes around.
*Ah waitin' for mih lil' sou sou hand to come 'round to buy mih new
stove.*

soucouyant (soo-koo-yah)
From the French *sucer,* meaning "to suck". A Trinidad folklore
character of a vampire that takes the form of an old woman in the
daytime, and as a ball of fire at night to prey on a person's blood.
Yuh skin bruise up like a soucouyant suck yuh.

soul case
The physical body.
Ah tired tellin' yuh doh bodder mih soul case. Me eh goin' no whey.

soursop
A fruit with a soft pulpy interior and a rough thick green skin. The
flavour is pleasant, and it is excellent for making icecream.
*Mih soursop tree now comin' good good. Soon Claude say is
soursop icecream fuh so.*

souse
A popular dish for Sunday brunch; made of pickled pork parts, and
served with cucumber, tomatoes and onions in the brine.
*Souse, black pudding an' coconut bake is mih favourite breakfast
back home.*

spirit lash
An event that occurs suddenly; an occurrence of something strange
and almost mystical.
Like yuh sufferin' from spirit lash since yuh lorse de case!

spit mih out
To disconnect.
Since yuh busy wit' yuh new boyfrien' is like yuh spit mih out.

Sprangalang
The name of a popular Trinidad emcee and comedian.
*Is Sprangalang self wha does make de commercial wit' de flour an'
roti.*

spread joy
To bring happiness to others, usually by distribution of money or some other form of gifts.
Ah did love when Uncle James arrive wit' he posse for Carnival to spread joy fuh so.

spread off / spread out / sprawl out / loll off
To extend oneself by lounging.
If yuh see how dem come an' spread off on mih new carpet.

squinge up / squingy
From the English *squint*, meaning "to close your eyes in bright light"; shrivelled up; close tightly.
Carol squinge up she eyes when ah tell she to smell de pepper sauce.

stand pipe
A roadside pipe, that was a popular meeting place in the old days.
Is by de stand pipe Miss Nettie meet Uncle Johnnie when she did move to Toco.

steelband
The orchestra engaged in beating notes on an oil drum.
We Trinis really eh begin to understand de steelband is a gem dat we give to de world!

steups (stee-oops) / cheups
A derogatory response to something distasteful or unacceptable, accompanied by a shrug of the head and shoulder.
When dem politicians talkin' plenty garbage me does jes steups an' turn off de TV.

stick fight
Inter-village rivalry in which men pit themselves against each other to become the champion stick fighter, accompanied by chants and taunts sung by chantwells.
When yuh did hear "bois" in dem days it did mean "wood" or "stick fight".

sting ray
A poisonous fish with spikes; a person with a fierce temper.
Doh tangle wit' Roslyn at all as she is a real sting ray.

stingy brim
A hat with narrow brim popular in the fifties.
Daddy still have dat stingy brim yuh see he wearin' in de photo album.

stinkin' toe
A large tree of the legume family, with pods bearing smelly seeds.
Doh pass dat nasty smellin' stinkin' toe pod by mih nose.

storm
To gate crash.
Watch how dem people go storm de fete since de security guard is dey friend.

string band
Musicians in a brass band of the forties and fifies; a family with many small children.
De Alacazar family in Tunapuna used to have de sweetes' string band for Christmas an Carnival.

suck eye
Easy; piece of cake.
Movin' dem cases of beer is suck eye for dem helpers preparing fuh de fete.

suck yuh teeth *(see* **steups***)*

sugar apple
A fruit with rough outer skin and white pulpy interior related to the
soursop but small and round.
Me eh know why we cyar see we sugar apple sellin' in de market.

sucrier (see-kee-ae)
From the French meaning "sugar bowl"; a very sweet type of banana.
Gimme de sucrier fig any day to dem other kinds of fig.

sugar cake
Candy made of grated coconut and boiled in sugar; a term of
endearment.
*"You are my sugar cake and honey plum" is what Pa write in he
love letters to Ma.*

sweet broom
A herb used for making bush baths to cure affliction; for *cooling.*
*Ah waitin' fuh yuh to put de sweet broom in de basin of warm water
fuh de chile bath.*

sweet drink
Any sweetened aerated beverage like Coca Cola or Solo; a non
alcoholic drink.
What yuh mean soda pop? Is sweet drink we does call it down here!

sweet eye
To wink while flirting.
David, doh let yuh wife ketch yuh making sweet eye at mih nuh!

sweet hand
The gift of cooking food that is tasty and mouth-watering.
Oh gorm Deb, yuh eh play yuh have sweet hand fuh so!

sweet man
A philanderer.
*Yuh fadder was one sweetman. No wonder yuh have so much
pumkin vine family!*

sweet oil
An expensive imported oil; used sparingly in making mayonnaise salad.
Ma used to put a little sweet oil in de mayonnaise salad to make it nice.

sweetie
A candy; a term of endearment.
A sweetie I did like when ah was growin' up was halay filay.

swell up yuh face
To pout and sulk showing ill-temper.
If yuh only swell up yuh face for me boy, ah go let you have one lash.

T

tabanca (tah-bank-ah)
A state of depression brought on by an unrequited love.
Keitos how come yuh listenin' to all dem period song so, yuh have tabanca or what?

tabanca music
Romantic music associated with past love affairs.
Whitney Houston really makin' mih feel to listen to some more tabanca music.

tac
The three jumps in a game of *tic tac toe*; to make a pass; to "tac back"' means to "double back".
Chile, is months now Ramesh makin' ah tac by me.

tadjah
Elaborate replicas of mausoleums built of bamboo and papier mache. It is paraded in the celebrations of the Muslim festival of Hosay.
Come chile leh we go dong St. James to see de tadjah an' dem.

take a bath
To shower; to take a dip in the ocean, river or swmming pool; to wash oneself at a standpipe.
Ah goin' to take a bath as ah feelin' hot an' sweaty.

take ah lag
To focus attention in correcting something or someone.
He comin' back home to take ah lag in mih tail.

take ah side
To align oneself with a group.
Look boy, take ah side in dis argument or go 'way.

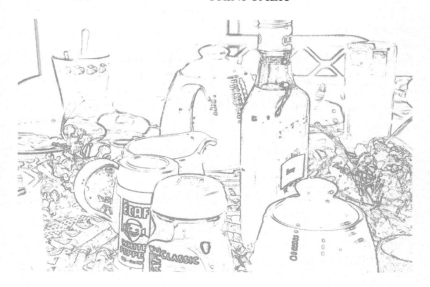

take 'way
To take away.
Take 'way de rest of de food from de table as ah lorse mih appetite.

talk tent
A place to hear Trini talk.
We always did look out for Keens-Douglas an' he talk tent for Carnival.

talkari (tal-kah-ree)
From the Hindi *tankaree*, meaning vegetables cooked as a hot, spicy and tasty accompaniment to rice or roti.
Drive past de Curepe roundabout headin' South yuh go start smellin' good talkari.

tam
An abbreviation for the Scottish *tam-o-shanter*, a little cap perched on the head, and was once a popular type of headwear.
Push back yuh tam a little. Now yuh lookin' reel snazzy.

tamadole
Tomato.
Tamadole cook down wit' onion an' pepper an' ting does nake a good choka to go wit' sada roti.

tamarind (tam-bran)
A brittle-shelled fruit; good in making delicacies like *chutney*.
Look at tamarind! Maurice say all yuh have a real gold mine dey!

tamboo bamboo
From the French t*ambour,* meaning "drum". Percussion drumming with lengths of bamboo was started at the turn of the 20th century after animal skin drums were banned.
Is tamboo bamboo what used to accompany stick-fightin' oui!

tanka lang / tah la la
A childish taunt to describe confusion; a misunderstanding.
When ah was small ah used to get in enough tanka lang.

tannia
A small round ground provision good in soups or accra.
Since ah turn vegetarian ah get to love tannia an' ting.

Tan Tan
From the French *tante,* meaning "aunt"; *Tan Tan* is the female character immortalized by Peter Minshall in his presentation of Saga Boy.
Is to see Tan Tan and Saga Boy in all dem big cities makin' we mas popular.

tantana
A creole word, meaning a lot of fuss.
Minshall dress up Tan Tan in plenty tantana.

tantie
From the French word *tante,* meaning "aunt"; a term of respect and endearment.
Tantie Merle was a funny character made famous by Paul Keens-Douglas.

tapia
The old-time Amerindian method of building with mud and straw; also the name chosen by Lloyd Best for his socio-political think-tank.
Yuh could always tell dem writers from Tapia when dem give yuh one setta big words.

tassa
The art of beating large drums during East Indian celebrations.
De tassa band section does always pull a big crowd on Carnival.

tasso
From the Spanish meaning "hard meat"; it was thought to be horse meat.
The meat ah buyin' from he tastin' like de tasso mih Grannie use to tell mih 'bout.

tattoo
An armadillo; one of the popular wild meats.
In all de wild meat is tattoo ah used to love de most.

tawa
From the Hindi meaning "baking iron".
Grease de tawa good as we eh want de roti to stick.

tay lay lay
A creole word meaning "worn out"; tattered clothes.
De chorus is "Ole lady walk a mile an' a half in she tay lay lay".

tea
Any hot beverage whether tea leaves, lime bud leaves, chocolate or coffee; any afternoon snack and drink.
The tea custom really come from de English who get it from Chinese people.

tears
A situation that is laughable or ridiculous to the extent that it could make one laugh or cry.
Dat girl is tears yes, look how she dress up cosquelle.

ten commandments
Ten toes.
A:*Yuh come back wit' yuh ten commandment on de ground?*
B: *Dey tief mih Reeboks!*

throw in de bamboo
To make someone vulnerable.
He eh get what ah write, so Peter say ah throw he in de bamboo.

tent
Originally the yard fenced with coconut branches where calypsoes were sung.
Mih wife used to love de calypso tent doh mind she was a real church post.

tess
A young male.
Dem tess used to come by we in Balandra to lime an' catch fish.

teta (tay-tah)
A fresh water fish with a wide mouth.
With she mout' like a teta she comin' to throw words over mih fence.

ti marie
From the patois *petite Marie,* meaning "little Mary"; the Trinidad name for "Sensitive Plant" or "Mimosa", a delicate but thorny plant that closes its leaves when touched.
Long time we used to sing to de ti marie an' when we touch de leaves it use to fold up.

tie tongue
One who speaks with a lisp; a speech impediment.
Doh mind he tie tongue he win all dem public speaking debates.

tie up
To confuse; to describe a state of marriage or dating.
In court he tie up heself wit' all dem lies he tell de magistrate.

tief
Thief.
Ah tired shout "tief" an' no police eh see or hear meh.

tilapia
A fresh water fish, introduced as a food source and a scavenger of mosquito larvae.
Dey used to breed tilapia by dem big pond in front Cipriani Labour College long time.

ting / ting ting
Thing; applied to any situation or person.
Freddie pick up wit' a nice little ting at de party.

ting up
Conceited; a pushy or overbearing attitude.
She too ting up wit' she self, dah is why nobody doh like she.

tinnin
Aluminium or zinc sheetings, used to cover buildings or to make
fences; also known as *galvanize.*
Ah get dis cut from a piece ah tinnin ah fall down on.

tizzic
To have a fit; to get convulsions; a nervous twitch.
*De whole country gorn into a tizzic wit' all dis bacchanal takin'
place.*

Tobago love
An unsual method of romancing from a distance; long-distance lovers.
*All yuh only correspondin' by email, is a case of Tobago love or
what?*

Tobagonian
A native of Tobago.
*Tobago is well known fuh its Buccoo Reef an' Nylon Pool as well as
fuh its curry crab an' dumpling, Tobagonian style.*

toe jam
An offensive odour given off from sweaty feet or dirty toes.
Ah cyar take dis toe jam no more so ah goin' an' bathe.

tolay halay nalay weyday
Apathetic.
He cyar be my chile, de boy too quiet an' tolay halay nalay weyday.

tone
The custom of giving jokes.
*Yuh know how ah doh like yuh to give mih tone 'bout de boy nex
door.*

tonka bean
A sweet sticky fruit, dried and used for flavouring.
Is ah long time since ah smell tonka bean dryin' out.

Tonnerre! (ton-neh)
From the French meaning "thunder"; an exclamation.
Tonnerre! It have plenty people inside dis fete!

topi tambo
Root tubers that taste like Chinese water chestnuts when boiled in salted water.
Ah stuff mih belly wit' enough topi tambo dis mornin'.

torchon (toe-shor)
From the French meaning "dish cloth"; fruit of a vine that becomes rough and fibrous when dried, like a natural bottle-brush.
Leave de torchon on de wire fence to dry out if yuh doh mind.

tote feelings
To carry a heavy mental burden.
Plenty of domestic violence cases is because dem men does be totin' feelings.

tot tots / tay tay
The childish name for a mother's breasts.
Since Elvis small he does like to lie on Mamee tot tots an' fall asleep.

tourne langue (toon lang)
From the patois meaning "to change tongue or speech"; to change the topic abruptly.
If yuh hear how he tourne langue when he know he was losin' de case.

toute bagai
From the French meaning "everything", all and sundry.
It have toute bagai in dis dress shop in Princes Town.

tout monde (tout moon)
From the French *tout le monde,* meaning "everybody".
Tout monde, come an' get de barbeque before it finish.

toutoulbé (too-tool-bay)
Incredibly stupid or love sick.
He really gone toutoulbay since he pick up wit' dat gyul las' Christmas.

town say (tong say)
To repeat a juicy piece of old talk; to verify a *mauvaise langue.*
Is town wha say dat is he self who really send she mad.

trackin'
In hot pursuit of love.
It eh today dat Joey trackin' Anisa nah!

travel
To go by route taxi or bus.
Mih car break down so ah had was to travel dis morning by yellow ban'.

travellin'
Dying.
When Tantie Bessie turn one hundred she was done already travellin'.

travesao / atravesao (tra-vay-sow)
From the Portuguese *atravesao,* meaning "light-skinned and of mixed descent".
Paolo is a travesao who lan' up from Brazil an' decide to turn Trini.

Trinbago (trin-bay-go)
The fusion of Trinidad and Tobago.
Pan Trinbago is de official national organization for all local steelband.

Trinbagoninan
A native of Trinidad and Tobago.
Dis is one time ah go call mihself Trinbagonian instead of Trini.

Trini (tree-nee)
A reference to someone who is Trinidadian by birth or by adoption; native in attitude and behaviour.
Dem tourists was winin' down de place like real Trini.

Trini Talk
A hybrid of languages from all corners of the globe but with a definite French influence on the English. It is unique and indigenous to Trinidad and Tobago, complete with sing song accent.
Dis Trini Talk sweet fuh so eh! Buh wait til yuh hear it on audio!

Trinidad time
To describe the fact that Trinidadians are usually late for everything.
He tell meh to meet him at seven o'clock, meanin' after seven-thirty Trinidad time. He go be late for he own funeral.

Trinidadian
An easy-going personality attributed to someone born or bred in Trinidad.
Dem Trinidadian could go any place an' make deyself at home!

Trou Macaque (troo ma-kak)
From the French meaning "monkey hole"; a place where monkeys lived, now a densely populated district in the hills east of Port of Spain.
From where Marvin live in Trou Macaque he say he could see Venezuela.

true true / in truth
Not to be doubted.
Dis ting really true true. She gorn an' marry de man in truth.

try ah ting
To make a pass; an attempt to start a love affair; to make a start .
Well give mih credit. Ah try ah ting on she, doh mind it eh work.

tulum / tulum bum bum
A dark sticky candy made of grated coconut cooked in molasses.
Is years now since ah eat ah good tulum bum bum.

turn ole mas
To turn everything into a confusion; a reference to *j'ouvert* characters
when the costumery is old and dirty.
*From de time dis man return from America he make everyting turn
ole mas in de family.*

turnkey (tun-kee)
A gaoler or one who holds the keys to prison cells; a prison officer.
Dem turnkey have dey hand full wid so many prisoners.

tush (toosh)
To touch lightly whether in a game of marbles, or in a car accident.
Watch yuh doh tush mih fender when yuh backin' out of de garage.

twenty four hours
A wood slave; another name given to the type of domestic lizard
which, though harmless, has a reputation of giving one only twenty
four hours to survive an "attack".
*It have plenty other name for de twenty four hours like de American
name gecko.*

two by four
Any ridiculously small place.
*It eh have no reason why we cyar find dem criminals in dis two by
four country.*

two twos
In a jiffy; in a hurry.
Doh worry! Ah comin' back to cook for all yuh in two twos.

U

under all de ole talk
To get down to the serious part of the discussion.
Under all de ole talk ah have to reach back home in time for de news.

under de trees
A liming spot at the Normandie Hotel in St Ann's.
Under de trees people does read wat dey write.

University of Woodford Square
Dr. Eric Williams delivered many memorable lectures on the state of the nation in Woodford Square.
We mus' do someting to celebrate de historic value of de University of Woodford Square.

up de broom
An old superstition that says when a broom is upended in a corner a visitor would soon take his leave.
Mama always did turn up de broom when she church people come fuh coffee an' didn't know when to leave.

up de road
Opposite to "down de road", with no fixed distance or direction.
Ah jes' goin' up de road to come back down later.

up in arms
Angry; to want to go to war with another.
He up in arms wit' de landlord who serve he eviction notice.

ups an' …
To arrive at a sudden decision; on the spur of the moment.
Pulmatee ups an' gorn down de road to buy a Bollywood DVD.

upset de ting
To disturb one's emotional equilibrium; to disturb the state of affairs.
After ah done make up wit' she yuh big mout gorn now an' upset de ting.

upside down
To be confused; adversarial.
All yuh children have mih vex at how yuh turn de house upside down.

upside down hotel
A reference to the Trinidad Hilton Hotel, where one goes down to one's room.
Is fete fuh so every ole year's night at de upside down hotel.

uses to
Used to.
Ma uses to take we to church every Sunday but now she dead we doh go no wey.

V

vagrant
A street dweller.
De Mayor really tryin' to clean up Port of Spain by movin' all dem vagrant.

vaps
A sudden or unexpected urge to do something.
Tantie stay jes' so an' ketch ah vaps an' start to wine dong de place.

vengeance of Moko (*see*** Moko)**

Veni Mange (vee-nee mah-jay)
From the French *venir manger,* "to come to eat"; also the name of a popular dining and liming spot.
Dey cyar stop a good Veni Mange lime wit' mih Roses an dem.

vert ti vert (vey-tee-veh)
Dried roots of a Trinidad grass used to perfume closets and dress hangers.
Yuh know mih mother clothes does still smell of vert ti vert!

vex
Vexed.
Doh go an' get mih damn vex here and make me mash up de place.

vicey
From the English meaning "vice" or "of corrupt nature"; in French *vice* means "depraved"; rude thoughts or actions.
Yuh tink ah coulda have vicey thoughts in mih head? Ah woulda have to go to confession pronto.

vieux causer/cosay (vieh-ko-zay)
From the French *vieux* meaning "old", and *causer* meaning "to chat"; the patois for *ole talk*; idle chatter.
Doh give mih all dat vieux causer 'bout de office comesse. Ah sick an' tired hearin' all dat chupidness.

vi ki vi
From the patois meaning "halfway"; incomplete; disorderly.
She does clean de place vi ki vi because she want to rush out an' lime.

village ram
A stud; a philanderer.
Yuh wouldna believe dat old man used to be de village ram long time.

Vincie (Vin-cee)
A native of St. Vincent.
Yuh could always tell a Vincie by de way he does speak jokey.

virus
Any common cold named according to whatever is topical at the moment.
Ah waitin' to see if dey go call dis latest cold virus de SOE.

vital supplies
A necessary amount of food requirements for one's survival.
Before yuh board de plane make sure yuh load up wit' vital supplies of Crix an' peppersauce.

vup (voop)
A term used in cricket when the batsman tries to hit the ball as hard as possible; a wide swing.
Doh go an' drop a vup on mih now.

W

wachekong (wash-ee-kong) (*see* **gym boots**)
Old-fashioned sneakers that were popular and practical for school children. One version with high backs around ankles were called *gym boots*. They were forerunners to present-day sneakers.
We uses to keep we wachekongs clean wit' whitenin' call "blanco".

wail / wail down
To cry and make loud noises. To dance, jump, prance, and be on the borderline of vulgar at Carnival time.
Is to see dem social people from Westmooring wail down de place in Carnival fetes.

wajang / wajank
A person of loose morals; lewd and unbecoming behaviour.
We mus' do someting 'bout all dem little wajang we breedin'.

wake
A social gathering at the home of the bereaved on the night of the news, accompanied by card playing, story-telling, coffee and *Crix*.
Leh we put up a tent outside for de crowd dat go gather for Percy wake tonight.

wappia (wah-pee-ah)
Saliva that settles in the corner of the mouth after too much talking.
Stop talkin' an'wipe de wappia from yuh mouth.

wappie
A card game of chance, played in yards or on the side walks for money.
Yuh still wastin' yuh money on dem wappie games?

Warahoon
A South American tribe in the Venezuelan jungle; wild looks and behaviour.
Melvina was fightin' up in de sale down town an' if you see how she was gettin' on like a Warahoon.

wash stand
The bedroom furniture that served as a utility toilet area for washing up.
If yuh see how much dem sellin' Grannie ole wash stand fuh in de antique shop!

wassie
Raucous behaviour; misbehaving; vulgar dancing.
If it was long time dey woulda say de pastor sister was behavin' wassie at de concert.

waste down (wase dong)
To finish; to wipe out, especially to gulp down food.
Mih half-brother gorn an' waste down de las' of mih groceries.

waste ah time
To expend energy on what is not worth the while.
Is a big waste ah time to make ginger beer as it eh go las' five minute.

water goblet (*see* **goblet**)

water nut
A young coconut.
Make sure to ask de coconut vendor fuh a water nut.

water wash
Clothes freshly washed and wrinkled.
Yuh cyar go to school wit' dat water wash uniform.

Wha' happen!
What has happened; an exclamation.
Wha' happen! Yuh never see a handsome man before!

whe whe (way way) / play whe
A game of chance, based on dreams and symbolic representations;
Play Whe is a national lottery.
Me eh care if is whe whe or play whe, yuh better go an' find back mih money.

whitey cockroach
A pale-faced person; a white man.
Doh mind if dey call yuh Whitey Cockroach eh Mr. Applegate, is only ah little heckle.

wild meat
Wild animals that are hunted for their meat.
It have laws to protect dem lappe an' manicou from all yuh people who does like to eat wild meat.

wind pies
Imaginary snacks.
Me eh have no change so is wind pies ah having for lunch.

wine
The gyrations, oscillations and other body movements from the hip.
Yuh grow up in Englan' so whey yuh learn to wine like dat?

winer gyul
A breed of female who can "wine like a ball of twine"; made famous in calypso.
Yuh gettin' on jes like de winer gyul from Princes Town.

wingy (win-gee)
A state of thinness that causes a man's pants to fit badly and to fold and pleat under his belt; an outfit that is odd and loose fitting.
Like yuh losin' weight Duncan. How come yuh pants fittin' so wingy?

wonder of the world
A Trinidad plant with thick succulent leaves, which grows roots when placed between pages of a book.
Ah never forget mih school days an puttin' wonder of de world inside mih book.

worm grass
A strong-smelling herb popular as a long-time remedy for purging intestinal worms.
All yuh children need a good dose of worm grass for de holidays.

wutless / wotless
A worthless person.
Wotless is de name dat Kes give to he 2011 Carnival album.

X

x / ex
To put a cross somewhere; to erase; an accelerator.
Doh mash de ex so hard, yuh go mash up de excelerator.

x in box
This is how many Trinidadian children still learn the final part of the
English alphabet.
*Yuh doh remember singin' "x in box" when Teacher Edith put we
under de mango tree?*

x-tray
X-ray.
Ah come to collect mih x-tray picture from de doctor.

Y

yam
A large food tuber with white interior and wiry rootlets; a popular ground provision and staple.
If yuh doh peel de yam good ah go have to throw yuh outta mih kitchen.

yampee
Mucus from the eyes; unclean eyes.
Wake up nah an' go wash de yampee from yuh eyes.

yankee dollar
American currency, made popular by American marines in WWII.
Calypsonians uses to sing 'bout prostitutes working fuh de yankee dollar.

yankee password
The F word.
All yuh big men eh shame to use dem yankee password in front de children!

yay yay fly
A bug; an irritating person; a cry cry baby.
Stop gettin' on like a yay yay fly an' do yuh homewuk.

Yes man!
A namby pamby; it can mean an affirmative.
Yes man! All ah we is one family.

yesterday self
"Self" is added for emphasis when speaking.
Is yesterday self ah see she limin' wit' de same good-fuh-nutten.

young fridge
Any large electronic speaker.
If yuh see how dem young fridge turn into master blasters on dem big mack trucks now!

yuh
You, or your.
Yuh is a chupidee. Yuh bold face too bad.

Z

Z (zed)
The last letter of the English alphabet; pronounced as "zed", not as the American "zee".
A: *Remember when we uses to sing zed for zebibull?*
B: *But gyul wha is a zebibull?*

zaboca
An avocado pear.
Dat zaboca perfect to go wit' pelau. It nice an' sticky an' yellow. Is a reel Pollock.

zabricot (zah-bree-koh)
A small type of mango.
Dis zabricot is ah sweet mango too bad!

Zaffaire yuh! *(zah-fey-yuh)*
From the patois meaning "that is your affair" or "to hell with you".
Yuh tink ah comin' to help? Zaffaire yuh!

zandolee
A small lizard that is extremely fast and elusive; a person with a zig zag nature.
Doh trust he nuh he does move like zandolee.

zeb a femme
From the French *herbes d'femmes,* meaning "herbs for women"; herbs for feminine problems.
Zeb a femme go set yuh right dis month so doh worry.

zeb a pique
From the French *herbes,* pronounced in patois *zeb;* a plant used to make a strong tea for curing abdominal pains.
Pick up a little zeb a pique on de way down from Tamana.

zi zi zeb (zee-zee-zeb)
A teenzy little being; a small native bird *picoplat* is called *ci ci zèbe.*
He was a little zi zi zeb jes de other day, now he's a big pappy an' chairman of de Board.

zig zag
A crooked person; a con man; a liar.
He cyar work wit' me at all. He too zig zag.

zog
An uneven cut made by a barber or hairdresser on a full head of hair.
Yuh head look like de barber zog up yuh hair.

zoot
Discarded stub of a cigarette.
Dem vagrant does collect all dem zoot .

zwill
Thin; one who looks under-nourished; a kite tail that is thin and long and used with razor blades to cut a competitor's kite.
She lookin' like a zwill an' remind mih of dem kite ah use to fly in de Savannah.

PROVERBS

Trini Proverbs

The Caribbean is noted for its quaint sayings and proverbs appropriate for any occasion. These sayings originated out of the need of the slaves to converse with each other in a language that could not be easily understood by their masters.

Because the language of the plantocracy was French, for many the new language combined bits of broken French and English with their own African dialects. The result was a patois rich in humour and mischievous with ridicule that spoke volumes in satire and wisdom.

The following proverbs or sayings are anglicised but will whet your appetite for the original patois versions.

For example, in patois: ***Depuis qui temps ca ca yeux qu'a changer place?*** In English it translates into "Since when yampee changes its place?" It means ***How incredible! That is certainly an unexpected turn of events!***

To those who are still in contact with patois this musical version is far more effective than its dilution into English. The following listing however recaps some of those popular sayings that remain with us today.

After one time is two time.
Look how things have changed! Once it was a certain way now look what has happened!

Ah better chalk yuh foot.
A display of welcome the first time someone visits one's home.

All skin teet eh ah laugh. / Not every skin teet is a laff.
Not every smile is genuine. Beware of treachery!

A still tongue keeps a wise head.
Think before one talks otherwise one can speak out of turn and attract trouble.

Blood thicker than water.
Family ties bind deeper and stronger than strangers'.

Bush have ears. / Walls have ears.
Be careful how one speaks as someone may be listening.

Corbeaux cyar eat sponge cake.
A low-class person has difficulty adjusting to a high-class position.

Crapaud smoke yuh pipe.
One will not be able to help oneself or get help from others.

Cut yuh style to suit your cloth.
Be practical and live within one's means; adjust to suit the occasion.

Dat and God face you will never see.
A curse that relegates the offender to the worst possible future.

Dat doh change de price of cocoa.
Nothing makes a difference with the state of affairs that one is in.

De eyes of de master fatten de calf.
Those working with one will perform better if one is around.

De longer you live is de more you learn.
The older one grows the wiser one becomes.

De longest day have an end.
Be patient. Everything will eventually be finished.

De longest rope have an end.
Never mind it seems unending but the situation will one day be over.

Do so eh like so.
Do unto others as you would have them do unto you.

Don't count your chickens before dey hatch.
It is folly to take things for granted.

Don't let your right hand know what yuh left hand is doing.
Keep everything close to one's heart; don't share secrets with anyone.

Don't trouble trouble unless trouble trouble you.
Don't interfere with problems, leave well enough alone.

Drop by drop does full bucket.
A little at a time in whatever one is doing will see one through.

Drunk or sober mind yuh business.
No matter what, take care of oneself first.

Empty bag cyar stand.
Without a full stomach, one cannot be expected to perform.

Everyday at your neighbour house eh good.
Familiarity breeds contempt.

Everything good to eat but everything not good to talk.
It is not everything one should expose in conversation.

For love nor money.
The futility of doing something.

Friends carry you away but dey doh bring you back.
Watch out for the company one keeps. Don't be misled by false friends.

God bless mih eyesight.
It is good to see you; it's been a long time; I'm so happy we meet.

God don't like ugly.
There is a higher power who will not tolerate wrong-doing and evil.

God is ah Trini.
Nothing bad will happen to Trinidad and Tobago because God is one of us.

God is not a Bajan.
There is justice after all as God does not have a nationality.

God wear pyjamas but He don't sleep.
Take heart; God is watching and will act.

Hurry dog eat raw meat.
A state of anticipation that could make you act stupidly and prematurely.

If de milk spoil in de morning throw it away.
Should one have a problem, deal with it early so that it won't worsen.

If you have cocoa in de sun, look out for rain.
If one has business that needs attention, one had better see about it, or else trouble might occur.

If you live long enough you go see de end of the world.
The longer one lives the more incredible life becomes.

If you play wit fire, you bound to get burn.
Be careful with living dangerously as one may pay the consequence.

Is who in de kitchen does feel de heat.
Those closer to the problems are the ones who undergo the most stress.

Jail eh make to ripe fig.
It shows no fear of "making a jail" or feeling shame.

Leave it at de foot of de cross.
Don't take on the problem; trust your faith and leave it to Jesus.

Like goat shit on hill when wind blow.
A comparison to someone who is overly sensitive and responds quickly as when wind blows around the small pebbles of goat faeces.

Nothing doh happen before its time.
Everything takes time and all will happen in due course.

One day for police, one day for tief.
You may be getting away with misdeeds but sooner or later you will get caught.

One day, one day, congotay.
Sooner or later the day of reckoning will arrive and then you will know!

Tief from tief make God laugh.
One who steals from a thief makes an amuzing situation.

Time longer than twine.
If you have patience it will come to pass.

To give your eye teet.
One will go to any extreme to acquire something desired.

Today for me tomorrow for you.
It may seem that my trouble will never end, but your turn will come.

To turn blood to water. / No more blood to give.
To harass another so that the person feels drained and tired.

You cyar chook down God with bamboo.
God is not there at your beck and call nor does He exist to fulfil your every whim and fancy.

Water more than flour.
The point at which something becomes too difficult to bear and something clearly has to be done.

When cock get teet.
Something that is impossible and will never happen.

You could take the man out of the gutter, but you can't take the gutter out of him.
It is difficult sometimes to instil good manners into someone who was not well brought up.

Pot cyar call de kettle black.
One is in no position to laugh at another if one is in a similar situation.

What dey give yuh to rub yuh eat.
A state of being seduced and disadvantaged.

Take a six for a nine.
To be misled and therefore conned into a silly situation.

Playing dead to catch corbeau alive.
To show humility to impress and therefore win out in the end.

Heat in yuh tail but you whistling.
To pretend to be okay when one is really hurting.

There is more in de mortar than de pestle.
There is more to it than meets the eye.

You doh ketch fly with vinegar.
One must be cunning and use "sweet talk" to get what one wants and not try harsh tactics.

Monkey doh see he own tail.
People are quick to criticise others unmindful of their own faults.

You cyar be ugly and bad lucky.
One can't be twice times unlucky; surely one must have something going for oneself.

What you expect from an empty bag of coals but dust.
Do not raise one's expectations; one can't make a silk purse from a sow's ear.

What don't kill does fatten.
If it doesn't kill one, chances are that one will live to overcome.

Only you know what cookin' in de pot.
Only the cook knows what he or she is doing; only the person in question knows the details of a personal situation.

What you do in de darkness bound to come to light.
Whatever undercover misdeeds one does will eventually be exposed.

Is trouble make monkey eat pepper.
Do not get oneself into hot water by looking for problems.

Words are wind, blows are unkind.
Ole talk does not matter, getting physical risks being abused.

What eye doh see, heart doh hurt.
What one doesn't know cannot hurt.

To chook out mih eye.
To take advantage of another.

Mih blood doh take yuh.
I do not like you.

Make sure better than cocksure.
Be sure of what one has rather than take things for granted.

Jigger foot clear de way, rock stone comin' down.
Be careful if one is vulnerable.

If push come to shove.
There may come the point at which one has no alternative to do otherwise.

Take in front before in front take you.
Plan ahead so that certain events don't overtake one.

What doh pass yuh doh miss yuh.
Be careful as it is not easy to escape one's Fate.

Who de cap fit, pull de string.
If what is taking place is of relevance to one, do something about it.

It take two hand to clap.
Only cooperation will help a situation; one cannot do it alone.

Spit out.
To detach and not have anything further to do with the matter.

Take it light. /Take it easy.
Go easy and do not ruffle oneself.

If you cyar catch Mammy, take Pappy.
To make do with what one has or the next best thing.

Makin' track for 'gouti to run on.
To make it easy for someone else to take advantage of one's work and claim the reward.

What eh meet you, eh pass you.
One will get one's just desserts sooner or later.

Gopaul luck eh Seepaul luck.
No two people are likely to share the same fate .

You cyar play mas an 'fraid mas powder.
One cannot get involved and not face the consequences, like the sailors who play mas on Carnival days teasing onlookers with powder.

Who doh hear does feel. / Who cyar hear go feel.
Those who don't take heed will learn the lesson the hard way.

Hard ears does feel.
If one continues to be stubborn without taking heed one will surely pay a price.

How you make your bed so you lie on it.
What you sow you shall reap.

When your neighbour house on fire you better watch your own.
Don't ignore what is happening around one as it could happen to one.

Sparrow does fly high but it must come down low to sleep.
Sooner or later one's big shot attitude will end and one will be humbled.

What is to is must is.
Fate has already decided what the future will be.

Monkey know what tree to climb.
One knows exactly what or who to take advantage of.

Is to beat de iron while it hot.
Take the opportunity to do something while it is in the creative stage so that one can shape it as one likes.

Don't bite de hand dat feed you.
One must not turn traitor to someone who has helped one in the past.

Never kick down de ladder you climb on.
Don't be foolish and destroy one's support.

Doh sit on de river bed and talk de river bad.
Don't malign someone who has helped you.

Don't damn de bridge you cross.
Be careful not to condemn the past; to show gratitude and respect to someone or something that has served one well.

Moon does run 'til day catch it.
One cannot run away from a particular situation forever.

Ah hear better cock than you crow.
I have heard people better than you brag, so I am not impressed with you.

Is not who you know, is who know you.
Do not trust "friends" as they may fail you. Better depend on those who remain faithful to you.

Fisherman never say de fish rotten.
A person with bad traits or defective goods usually won't admit to the fact.

Beating his own drum and dancin' to it.
An unrepentant braggart.

Never see come see.
A show-off who reacts childishly to unaccustomed good luck.

Ah cyar go nor come.
An expresssion of despair meaning the situation is irreversible.

Doh hang yuh hat where you cyar reach.
Don't be overly ambitious and money-greedy.

Two man rat cyar live in de same hole.
Two persons cannot issue orders at the same time from the same place. Power cannot or rather does not like to be shared.

You never miss de water 'til de well run dry.
Go on and take things for granted. One day it will be too late and only then one will appreciate what one had.

Monkey see monkey do.
Some people always follow the latest fad.

If de priest could play who is we?
If the priest could play mas how could I be wrong to do the same?

How dee an tan-kee break no bones.
It does not cost anything to have some good manners.

Shroud eh have pocket.
When one dies one cannot take one's earthly possessions.

Spit in de sky, it go fall back in yuh eye.
Wrong deeds will return to confront one.

Bambye you go see am.
To predict the way a marriage or a relationship will end adversely.

Ole firesticks easy to ketch.
Former lovers can easily have their flame rekindled with new passion.

You cyar make love on hungry belly. / No money no love.
It takes more than love to sustain a relationship.

Doh meddle in husband an wife affairs.
One shouldn't interfere in a close relationship and will mend without outside help.

What sweet in goat mouth sour in he bam bam.
It may start off beautifully but end up badly so one had better watch it.

Tongue and teet does have their ting.
However close two people are there must be some difference in opinion at times.

See me and come live with me two different things.
There are differences between being a visitor and being a roommate.

Every bread have its piece of cheese.
Everyone has a partner who agrees or sees eye to eye with the other.

Man gone man dey. / It have plenty fish in de sea.
If one has lost a lover, there are others to choose from.

De blacker de berry de sweeter de juice.
An allusion to the sexual competence of black people.

Little axe does cut down big tree.
A small man can achieve great success.

She's in de family way.
In a state of pregnancy.

Chop in water doh leave mark.
To do the deed without leaving evidence.

Everyday bucket go in de well one day it will stick.
Do not push one's luck without taking precautions.

It takes two to make a row.
It is the answer that starts the quarrel.

Don't take ah man by he looks. / Don't judge a book by its cover.
Don't judge by appearances only.

Everyday is de same khaki pants. / Same ole, same ole.
Boredom sets in with repetition.

Bend de tree when it start to grow.
Discipline one's children when they are young or else it will be too late.

Goat doh make sheep.
One does not bring forth children unlike oneself.

Guinea hen doh make ram goat.
There are more similarities than differences between one and one's children.

De fruit doh fall far from de tree.
Like father like son; like mother like daughter.

You doh pelt down green mango.
It is more common to criticise those who are performing than those who do nothing.

What is joke for school boy is death for crapaud.
What may seem quite funny to one is quite serious for the other.

Better nigger belly full dan good food waste.
Try to eat up everything rather that let it go to waste.

Better yuh mind old clothes than people business.
Mind one's own affairs.

You'd better pull up yuh socks.
Know one's place and have some respect.

Better to be an old man's darling than a young man's slave.
There is merit to having an older man in one's life who respects one than a younger man who is abusive.

Is today for you tomorrow for me.
Don't worry about me. I'll get satisfaction when my turn comes.

Monkey say cool breeze.
You'll get what's coming for you.

Is de change from de dollar that bring de noise.
It is the response in an argument that could start the big row.

Cut eye doh kill.
It doesn't matter how mad you are with me, I won't budge at all.

Cockroach have no right in fowl party.
Stay out of matters that don't concern you.

Dat beat all cockfight!
You've gone overboard. That is too much.

Eat de bread de devil knead.
To experience extremes of hard times.

De devil and he wife fightin' for a hambone.
When there is rumbling thunder, the devil is angry with his wife.

When you blight wet paper will cut you.
When one is unlucky even a lucky break will go wrong for one.

Money doh grow on trees.
It is not easy to earn money.

Doh put water in your mouth to talk.
Don't be afraid to tell it like it is.

Mouth open story jump out.
With a little encouragement everything comes out.

Giving me basket to carry.
To deceive someone while fooling with nice words.

Doh cut off yuh nose to spoil yuh face.
Don't risk losing face. Watch being too generous.

Dictionaries

1. The American People's Encyclopedia, Chicago Spence Press Inc., 1961.
2. The Bantam New College Spanish and English Dictionary.
3. Cassell's French/English Dictionary
4. The Concise Oxford Dictionary, Oxford, New York. Oxford University Press, 1990.
5. The Concise Oxford Dictionary of Proverbs, Oxford, New York, Oxford University Press, 1982.
6. Heinemann English Dictionary, London Heinemann Educational Books, 1979.
7. The Random House Dictionary of the English Language, New York, Random House, 1973.
8. Smaller Slang Dictionary, London, New York, Routledge, 1964.
9. Webster's New Collegiate Dictionary, London, 1960.

Bibliography

1. Ahye, M., *Golden Heritage. The Dance in Trinidad and Tobago*, Port of Spain, Heritage Cultures Ltd., 1978.
2. Anthony, M., *Towns and Villages of Trinidad and Tobago*, Port of Spain, Circle Press, 1988.
3. Brereton, B., *A History of Modern Trinidad 1783-1962*, Kingston, Port of Spain, London, Heninemann, 1981.
4. Ffrench, R., *A Guide to the Birds of Trinidad and Tobago*, Valley Forge, Harrowood Books, 1976.
5. Hill, E., *The Trinidad Carnival*, U.S.A., University of Texas Press, 1972.
6. Mendes, J. *Cote Ci Cote La*, Port of Spain, 1986.
7. Mavrogordato, Olga., *Voices in the Street*, Port of Spain, Inprint Caribbean Ltd., 1977.
8. Mahabir, N. and Manhabir, S. ,*Trinidad Hindi*, Chaka Publishing Co., 1990.
9. Quevedo, R., *Atilla's Kaiso* Trinidad, U.W.I. Extra Mural Studies, 1983.
10. Rajnarinesingh, M. and Shah, R., *Fetes and Festivals in Trinidad and Tobago*, Port of Spain, Trinidad Express/Inprint, 1991.
11. Retout, Sr. M.T. *Parish Beat*, Port of Spain, Inprint Caribbean Ltd., 1976.
12. Rohlehr, G., *Calypso and Society in pre- Independence Trinidad*, Port of Spain, 1990.
13. Solomon, D., *The Speech of Trinidad – A reference grammar*, Trinidad, U.W.I. School of Continuing Studies, 1993.
14. Yawching, D., *Who's Who and Handbook of Trinidad and Tobago*, Port of Spain, Inprint Caribbean Ltd., 1991.

Printed in Great Britain
by Amazon